BEND
BEER

BEND BEER

A HISTORY OF BREWING IN CENTRAL OREGON

JON ABERNATHY

Foreword by Gary Fish

To Bob and Kay —

Cheers!

AMERICAN PALATE

Published by American Palate
A Division of The History Press
Charleston, SC 29403
www.historypress.net

Cover photo courtesy of Gina Schauland. Image of bucket of hops on back courtesy of Deschutes Brewery.

First published 2014

Manufactured in the United States

ISBN 978.1.62619.467.0

Library of Congress CIP data applied for.

For my wife and kids, without whose patience this book may not have come to be.

CONTENTS

Foreword, by Gary Fish   9
Preface   13
Acknowledgements   17

1. Beer on the Frontier: Saloons, Isolation and Homesteads
   on the High Desert   21
2. Prohibition on the High Desert   35
3. Timber Town: The Boom Years   51
4. Recreation and Tourism   59
5. Laying Foundations: Deschutes Brewery and Other Pioneers   69
6. The Second Wave   101
7. The Brewery Explosion and the Rise of Beer Tourism   125
8. Beer Town, USA   137

Appendix. Timeline   149
Bibliography   159
Index   165
About the Author   173

FOREWORD

In 1987, Bend was still emerging from *the* great recession—no, not the recent one (in 2008). Many who were there suggest that the recent one was much milder than the recession of 1982. We were looking for a nice town to open a little pub, make some good beer and good food and have a nice life. No one could have predicted what would happen next.

Jon Abernathy does a wonderful job of telling the stories of not only the breweries but also the communities in which these breweries participated. When we opened Deschutes Brewery, we did some research and found that, although Deschutes was the first brewery in Bend, there had been a brewery (maybe more?) in Prineville just thirty miles away. However, we did not know the background of that brewery or the people involved. Jon's research puts us there in this community, isolated from the Willamette Valley and the more commercial brewing concerns that were there. Basically, in Central Oregon, if you wanted beer, you pretty much needed to make it yourself, or at least have it made close to you.

The craft beer movement in America is one of rebellion, entrepreneurship, passion, frustration and an unwillingness to accept the status quo. It is also a movement of and by the consumer. These consumers have steadfastly refused to accept the attempts of global manufacturers to tell them what products they need. This has played itself out in the wine renaissance in California, Oregon and beyond. It has also played itself out in coffee, cheese, produce and so on. In beer, those of us who were lucky enough to be involved with the genesis of American craft beer have tried only to

Gary Fish draws a glass of Cascade Golden Ale. *Photo by Chris Huskinson. Courtesy Deschutes Brewery.*

serve this consumer. Maybe we did not always understand it as such, but when the first homebrewers tried to take their hobby and their passion to a commercial level, the risk was that a consumer might not be there to sustain their business model. Fortunately, time has proved that there is not just *a* consumer but millions of them.

As Deschutes Brewery grew, the great stories from my perspective were always around the people who came here to make beer. We were lucky to associate with some very talented brewers who stayed with us for a while, many moving on to run their own breweries, expressing their own artistic perspectives on our bootstrapping industry. Again, the people are there helping to create this incredible brewing community in Bend and Central Oregon.

This book documents the struggles and the triumphs. It also documents the history of the people and the region that attracted us all to beautiful Central Oregon. Sometimes not knowing that a thing cannot be done is the greatest empowerment. We are lucky to be here, and we are happy you are coming with us through this book.

Cheers!

GARY FISH
Founder of Deschutes Brewery

PREFACE

When commissioning editor Aubrie Koenig of The History Press first approached me about writing a book on the history of beer in Bend, it took no time at all to say yes, although I have to admit that I would not have predicted *Bend Beer* would be my first book. Why? Simply put, it would be entirely correct to say that the history of beer in Bend *starts* in 1988 with Deschutes Brewery; and while there's certainly nothing wrong with writing about the breweries that have sprung up over the past quarter century, the end result is more guidebook than history. People were certainly drinking beer here since the town was little more than rye fields and cow paths, but Bend is a young city (incorporated in 1905) and simply does not have the brewing history and traditions of other beer regions like Portland, San Francisco, Milwaukee, St. Louis and so on.

Extending the net farther out into the rest of Central Oregon, we find that Prineville, settled three decades before Bend, had two frontier breweries between 1882 and 1906. And I even uncovered a few tantalizing yet unsubstantiated clues about a possible brewery located at Tetherow Crossing, a fording point on the Deschutes River used by travelers heading east after crossing the Cascade Mountains. That brewery, if it existed, likely would have been operational during the 1890s. (Unfortunately, there simply was not enough evidence to warrant a mention of this possible brewery, except where I could slip it into this preface.)

And of course, there were the saloons—the mainstay of any frontier town—and Prohibition, which invariably touches any beer-related history of a region in our country. So there I had my structure: start with the breweries of Prineville, survey the early saloon and beer landscape of the frontier, cover the history and effects of Prohibition on the region and examine beer's role in Bend's growth as a mill town and as tourism took over. Then I could pick up with Deschutes Brewery in 1988 and the growth of the beer culture that would eventually lead to Bend being referred to as "Beer Town, USA" in recent national media articles. Along the way, I could sprinkle in some of the key historical background of the region. So, what you have in your hands is certainly a beer book but also, I hope, one that a reader interested in the general history of Bend will pick up.

I've lived most of my life in Central Oregon, and I have been homebrewing and drinking craft beer since the '90s (back when we still regularly called it "microbrew"). My first "official" craft beer was one I ordered on my twenty-first birthday at Stuft Pizza in downtown Bend—I don't actually remember specifically what it was, probably something from Deschutes or one of the Portland breweries of the time. The first craft beer I drank that actually registered as something special was Widmer Hefeweizen, on tap at Ichabod's North in Spokane, Washington (where I spent college time during the mid-'90s). I was hooked, and I received much of my early craft beer education immersed in Spokane's craft beer scene—brewpubs like Fort Spokane Brewing, Birkebeiner Brewing, Voodoo Brewery, the Viking Bar (with something like four hundred bottled beers on the menu) and Jim's Homebrew Supply (both for homebrewing and its selection of bottled beers). Upon returning to Bend, I got involved with the local homebrew club at the time—meeting people like Tyler Reichert and Larry Johnson, who would go on to start their own brewery ventures—and (re)acquainted myself with the region's three (*three!*) breweries.

Throughout it all, I've been making websites in one form or another and codifying my thoughts on beer on them in what I suppose you could call a proto-blog format for nearly as long. In the early 2000s, I created actual blogs on which I've been writing about beer and Bend (and many other topics) for more than a decade. My beer blog, "The Brew Site," is the longest-running beer blog in the country, and because of that site, I've met many people and made many friends in the beer industry—brewers, both pro and home; publicans; writers and bloggers; marketers; distributors; and more. One constant I've encountered among everyone in the industry is the community spirit; everyone is nice, generous with their time and helps one another out. Or as Dogfish Head Brewery's Sam Calagione has famously said, "[O]ur industry is 99 percent asshole free."

This is especially true of the Central Oregon beer community, and I couldn't be more pleased to have my own small role in that and to have been given the opportunity to write this book on it.

ACKNOWLEDGEMENTS

Although it seems like writing should be a solitary activity, it turns out that no one writes a book alone, and this one was no exception. Throughout this process, there were many people who contributed invaluable input—without them, this book may not have come to be or would have been a different beast.

First and foremost, I need to thank Aubrie Koenig, my first commissioning editor at The History Press, who initially reached out to me about writing a book in the first place. Without her, none of this would have happened, and she offered early insight and advice that helped to shape the overall outline of what I eventually hammered out. In that vein, I must also thank my other History Press commissioning editor, Becky LeJeune, who ably and patiently helped to see this book to fruition.

Of course, without my family at home being patient, encouraging, cajoling and understanding during this process, there wouldn't be a book. Or it would have taken four times as long to write. My wife, Sherri, early on said to the kids, "We're not going to see Dad for six months," and while this turned out not to be entirely true, there were many evenings and weekends I spent researching and writing and being generally scarce. Sherri was diligent about kicking me into the office to work and was also the first-review reader of the various drafts, providing good feedback along the way. My kids, Kaitlyn and Brandon, were great about my overall absence, helped with opinions on possible book cover photos and generally took it all in stride.

Special thanks go to the various beer folks who made time in their schedules for interviews (in order of interview date): Tyler Reichert, Chris Justema, Tonya Cornett, Jimmy Seifrit, Chris Cox, Garrett Wales, Wade Underwood, Brett Thomas, Gary Fish, Clay and Melodee Storey, Brian McMenamin, John Harris, Mike "Curly" White, Ty Barnett, Tony Lawrence and James Watts. There were also a number of folks I spoke with or e-mailed who helped along the way, including Wendi Day, Chad Kennedy, Larry Johnson, Paul Arney, Larry Sidor, Paul Evers and a good number of others I'm sure I'm forgetting. I know I missed a number of people, which I'm sorry about, so I'm hoping for a second, longer edition so I can expand on their stories as well.

A number of people read through my drafts at various stages and provided feedback, suggestions and criticism that improved the book immensely. My brother Ben Abernathy was the first (besides Sherri) to critique my drafts, and his advice was crucial. Ben has been editing comics for years (definitely a dream job!), so he knows his stuff. Big thanks as well to Sandi Carrington, who has an eye for typos that others miss and provided a necessary reminder and correction to a piece of Sisters brewing history that I missed; Paul, Sandi's husband, offered his own special brand of blunt feedback. Mark Lindner, the "Bend Beer Librarian," provided excellent, constructive criticism for some sections with which I had been struggling, fact-checked me and made me think (and rethink) about others. Sara Thompson, Mark's wife, helped me to bring additional clarity to awkward sections that surely would have left readers scratching their heads.

I cannot express enough thanks to Gina Schauland for her fantastic photography (which graces the cover!) and patience through this process as I kept bugging her for more. Additional thanks go to Deschutes Brewery's founder Gary Fish for providing the foreword to this book, which seemed only fitting considering the influence that Deschutes has had on our brewing scene over the years. And while I'm on the topic of Deschutes Brewery, I must gratefully tip my hat to Jen Orlando, who was indispensable in providing some early photographs of the brewery, Gary Fish and John Harris.

Both the Deschutes Historical Society and the Crook County Historical Society were very helpful in my quest to pull together older historic photos that were relevant to the source material, and additional research time at the Des Chutes Historical Museum proved indispensable. The two photos of the Prineville breweries are courtesy of Crook County's Bowman Museum in Prineville proper, and the others are courtesy of the Deschutes Historical Society (thank goodness for scanned and indexed photos!). Everyone I worked with at both societies was gracious and helpful, and if you get a chance to become a member of either one, I would highly recommend it.

Of course, there were many others who provided help or a kind word along the way. Beer writer Brian Yaeger (author of *Red, White and Brew* and the new *Oregon Breweries*), currently living in the Netherlands, is just an e-mail away and provided general advice from time to time. *Portland Beer* author Pete Dunlop has been through this process before and was generous with his thoughts. James Jaggard, manager of Wanderlust Tours here in Bend, was quick to give me permission to run a stunningly great photograph of Cascade Lakes beers in a mountain lake, as well as any others I might need. Dolly Dyer-Haney over at the Growler Guys cheerfully put up with my picture taking and generally helped to keep me in beer. John Richen with McMenamins has been a great help, setting up the interview with Brian McMenamin and facilitating the procural of additional fantastic photos of the Old St. Francis School. My parents, Diane and Jon, and my other brother, Chris, offered much support and encouragement along the way and weighed in on cover photo options as well.

Nearly all of this book was written on evenings and weekends because I, like many (if not most) other authors, have a day job that pays the bills. There were times when I needed to adjust my work schedule for interviews, meetings, research and whatnot, and my bosses, Doug Simmons and Mark Knowles, were flexible and accommodating as necessary. Much appreciated!

Finally, a resounding thank-you goes to all the brewers and breweries that have chosen to call Central Oregon home. A lot of beer flows through the taps here, without which there simply wouldn't be much beer history to write about, much less beer to drink!

CHAPTER 1

BEER ON THE FRONTIER

SALOONS, ISOLATION AND HOMESTEADS ON THE HIGH DESERT

When one surveys the Bend, Oregon beer landscape in 2014, it would be understandable to assume the existence of a long and rich history. Deschutes Brewery, founded in 1988, is the fifth-largest craft brewery in the United States. Bend alone is home to eighteen brewing operations (Central Oregon as a whole claims twenty-six), earning the nickname "Beer Town, USA" in popular media. Breweries such as 10 Barrel and Boneyard are among the fastest growing in the state of Oregon.

More than a century before Deschutes Brewery was founded, however, the Central Oregon landscape was markedly different. Bend didn't exist—it was summer range country for vast herds of livestock driven from the eastern steppe. Prineville was the region's economic and political center, the largest outpost on the edge of a vast swath of open range. The ranch country of Sisters had been established as military outpost Camp Polk in 1866 and was the gateway to the Willamette Valley over the Cascade Mountains. The region was pockmarked with small towns destined to become ghost towns by the mid-twentieth century; other cities that would be prominent in 2014 were not even established yet.

This was the frontier, one of the last true frontiers of the American West, and through the end of the nineteenth century and the early years of the twentieth, it was a remote and hard, often desolate, country of ranchers, stockmen, miners, buckaroos, farmers, settlers and land-seekers drawn to the region by the promise of finding new land, establishing homesteads and starting new lives on the frontier. Most of Central and Eastern Oregon was open range, government land peppered with ranches on which freely ran thousands of head of livestock (both cattle and sheep), with waypoints few and far between. It was remote: until 1900, the nearest railroad point from Prineville was at The Dalles on the Columbia River, 120 miles distant, and travel into Central Oregon took days over rough terrain. Roads were all but nonexistent, the most developed being little more than rutted trails. In many ways, it was lawless. Range wars were common, particularly between cattle and sheep men, and gunfighters and vigilantes ran reckless in the towns. Killings were common. More than one citizen of the time was surely thankful that they were able to "dodge all the bullets that flew around the streets in Prineville."

The first permanent settlers to Central Oregon arrived in the Ochoco country of Crook County in 1867, establishing their log cabin settlement near the mouth of Mill Creek—about eight miles east of present-day Prineville. The following spring, as if to punctuate the hardships and dangerous reality of living on the frontier, the settlement was raided by Indians, its first log cabin was burned and supplies were stolen. Three of the six settlers who were present (the others being in the Willamette Valley at the time, preparing to bring their families east) escaped the raid unharmed, though without guns, food or shelter. They fashioned fake rifles out of willow sticks and marched west to the Warm Springs Indian reservation and from there over the Santiam Pass to their Willamette Valley homes to report on the raid on the settlement.

Indian raids notwithstanding, the settlement of Central Oregon proceeded; the first school was established that same year, 1868, at the settlement on Mill Creek. That was also the year Barney Prine established his ramshackle home, blacksmith shop, store and (later) saloon out of juniper logs on the bank of the Crooked River, giving his name to what would become the town of Prineville. Prine's store became a popular stopping place for riders on the open range, and as the ranching and stock communities in the area grew, so did the town; the first post office was established in 1871, and in 1877, the first plat for the city was filed, officially founding Prineville (although it wasn't until 1880 that the city was incorporated by the state and a city council was named). The frontier town thrived and became the economic center for trade and business for one hundred miles around, and when Crook County was formed in 1882, Prineville became the county seat.

By the end of that year, Prineville, then in existence for fourteen years since Barney Prine erected his home, had all the amenities a frontier town could need: hotels, livery stables, stores and markets, blacksmiths, sawmills,

Unidentified women on horseback in front of the Ochoco Brewery, circa 1884. *Courtesy Bowman Museum, Prineville, Oregon.*

churches, schools, newspapers, a flourishing saloon business and, of course, a brewery.

While it might seem surprising to encounter breweries in frontier America, outside the larger cities, in fact, they were quite common, and beer was often the preferred drink when available. According to Gary and Gloria Meier in their book *Brewed in the Pacific Northwest*:

> *Although the major Eastern breweries did good business in the Northwest, many mining, logging, and farming towns had their own breweries soon after they were founded. Because road and rail systems were in their infancy, and beer kegs were heavy and bulky, distribution of the early beers was restricted to small geographical areas. As a result, new breweries sprang up like mushrooms during the 1860s and 1870s. A further factor in this growth was the advent of local hops and barley cultivation around 1865. Before that, hops and malt had to be shipped to the Northwest from San*

Francisco. With the proliferation of breweries, peaking in the late 1870s, each city and town proudly boasted its own local beer.

Beer was sold in the saloons and also in "beer gardens," which sold nothing but beer. Despite the expression often heard in "B" westerns— "Whiskey, bartender, and leave the bottle"—in real life Westerners swallowed considerably more beer than the hard stuff.

There were actually quite a large number of frontier breweries in Oregon, and in many cases, a town had more than one. One finds breweries in Albany (three), Astoria (four), Baker City (three), Burns (two), Canyon City (one), Jacksonville (two), Lakeview (one), Pendleton (four), Roseburg (two) and The Dalles (two)—among many others, including Prineville, which itself hosted two breweries during this time.

In 1882, the Ochoco Brewery was established at Fourth Street and Main Street—Central Oregon's first. There is some question about who the first business owner was, for although the lot the brewery was built on was sold to Ed Evans and Asa Miles in August 1882 by Frank Loacker, several sources list Loacker as brewery owner from 1882 until 1884. (Meier and Meier actually refer to Loacker as "Locher"; however, the 1880 U.S. Census indicates that "Loacker" is the correct spelling.) A brewer himself, it is entirely possible that Loacker was involved with the brewery until late 1884, when Evans's and Miles's names were first associated with the brewery business, listed in an advertisement in a local newspaper as the proprietors, who were "now making better beer than ever before." Loacker himself was born in Austria in 1849 and came to Prineville sometime prior to 1880.

In December 1887, the Ochoco Brewery was destroyed in a fire—a total loss. Shortly thereafter, Asa Miles purchased a building that was formerly a carpentry shop, moved it to the burned brewery site and converted it to become the new brewery. This did not last long, however, for in 1890, Miles closed the brewery and sold the lot to C.C. Maling; the building later became the Buckhorn Saloon. Evans later considered reopening the brewery and was briefly in negotiations to buy the Buckhorn to do so, but nothing seems to have come of that.

Prineville's second brewery (and its last for more than a century) was the Prineville Brewery, established in about 1893 by George O'Neil on Main and Sixth in a building that was formerly a sawmill, built two years earlier. O'Neil and his brother, Walter, also owned and operated the O'Neil Saloon on Main Street between Third Street and Fourth Street, later adding a

Flooding of Ochoco Creek in Prineville, circa 1900; the Prineville Brewery is in the background. *Courtesy Bowman Museum, Prineville, Oregon.*

warehouse around the corner on Fourth Street. An 1895 ad for the O'Neil Saloon promised beer for five cents a glass.

In 1894, O'Neil was joined at his brewery by John Geiger, who became the brewer and co-proprietor. Geiger was a German brewer born in 1864 who immigrated to the United States in 1883. He appeared to be the active partner in the brewery, not only brewing "A1 Beer," which promised to be "[c]onstantly on tap and for sale by the keg," but also cutting and storing ice (an important part of any frontier brewing operation), which was also used by the O'Neil brothers. When he retired from the Prineville Brewery in 1906, that appears to have been the end of the brewery, as the O'Neils also sold their retail interests that same year.

Since the O'Neils owned both the Prineville Brewery and their own saloon, it would seem likely that they would have sold Geiger's A1 Beer, although no direct mention of this seems to appear in the ads of the time. Perhaps the beer advertised for five cents per glass in 1895 is Geiger's A1. In a 1905 advertisement for their saloon, it is claimed that they were the "Sole Agents for Hop Gold Beer," the popular brand from the Star Brewery in Vancouver, Washington.

Both the Ochoco Brewery and Prineville Brewery offered their beers on tap at their respective establishments, as well as for distribution. "Country orders" were solicited and fulfilled, and it's not difficult to imagine each doing a lively business in the community for people thirsty for fresh local beer. Indeed, in 1901, it was reported that Geiger had received a load of 150-gallon beer barrels with which he planned to "flood the town" with beer in the summer.

There was, of course, plenty of other beer to be found as well, both national and regional. Advertisements from the time offer up the promise of Schlitz, Rainier, Budweiser, the aforementioned Hop Gold Beer, the "celebrated ABC Beer" and the "famous Olympia Bottled Beer," which sold for twenty-five cents per bottle at Smith & Cleek's Reception Saloon.

If Prineville could be considered an outpost on the edge of the frontier (which it was), then the area soon to become Bend was considered the hinterlands. The upper Deschutes country—following the Deschutes River through the vast pine forests, rocky lava lands, cinder buttes and ancient volcanoes—was empty, untamed country through which the cattle men would drive their stock on their way to their summer range in the mountains. The late 1870s saw the first filings for homesteads in the area, and one of the first was the establishment of the Farewell Bend Ranch in 1877 by John Y. Todd, from which Bend derived its name.

Todd's Farewell Bend Ranch was located on the bend in the Deschutes River, where later the Brooks-Scanlon sawmill would be established and where the Old Mill District shopping center is located today. Todd was a colorful character in the history of the Oregon frontier: as a cattleman in Oregon's Tygh Valley, he began the successful operation of packtrains to the Idaho goldmines, and in 1860, he diverted that project into building the first bridge over the Deschutes River at Sherars Crossing (named for the man who later purchased it)—a toll bridge that effectively opened Central Oregon for settlement. Todd later moved his cattle and holdings south to the Farewell Bend Ranch, and following a disastrous 1880 cattle drive to Wyoming that effectively bankrupted him, Todd sold the Farewell Bend Ranch to John Sisemore in 1881.

Sisemore's Ranch competed with William Staats's own frontier outpost as a stopping point for travelers through the region; Staats's homestead was located only about a mile down the river (approximately where Drake Park is located today) and, in addition to lodging, offered up fresh vegetables in the summer thanks to Staats's irrigated garden. The two also competed over the name and post office of the region: Sisemore established the first

The Alexander Drake property, overlooking the Deschutes River. *Courtesy Deschutes County Historical Society.*

post office in 1886 under the name of "Bend" (the "Farewell" portion was removed by the government to avoid confusion with a Farewell Bend on the Snake River to the east), which lasted until 1899, when Staats successfully applied to become postmaster and changed the name to the one he favored, "Deschutes." This post office lasted until 1906, although relatively few people actually referred to the area under that name (and the "Bend" post office itself was reestablished in 1904).

The area of Bend was still little more than a scattered community of homesteads and stock country when Alexander Drake and his wife arrived in 1900 and decided to settle there (that year's U.S. Census population count: twenty-one). Drake, a midwestern entrepreneur, was interested in the irrigation and land development possibilities that the region offered, and news spread quickly that a "capitalist from the East" had arrived with plans to develop the remote cattle country. The Drakes purchased much of William Staats's property on the river and built their lodge at what is now the top of Drake Park in Bend's Mirror Pond parking lot. In 1904, Drake filed the official plat for the town, and on January 4, 1905, the city of Bend was officially recognized and incorporated.

Despite Bend's fast-paced growth—from a small community of homesteads and being described in 1902 as little more than "just a rye field with the old road running kitty-corner to it" to a 1903 population of 258 and then a population surge to 500 by 1905—the town was still very much on the

Bond Street in Bend, notorious for its saloons and houses of ill repute. *Courtesy Deschutes County Historical Society.*

Interior of the Log Cabin Saloon. *Courtesy Deschutes County Historical Society.*

edge of the frontier. The region's economic center, Prineville, was forty miles and a full day's travel away. Growth was spurred on by the development and promise of irrigation, new land and timber, and new arrivals meant thirsty drinkers, which naturally heralded the establishment of that old frontier stalwart: the saloon.

The demand was there, and the saloons did a lively and rowdy business; as Bend's growth continued unabated, the number of saloons grew along with it. A March 1903 editorial in the *Bend Bulletin* noted that "when Bend becomes a goodly-sized town the saloon is bound to come, among others, as a necessary evil," and by the fall of that year, there were two saloons. By 1905, the town had eight saloons and a "lusty red light district" on Bond Street. (Wall Street was the heart of the downtown district and the main north–south thoroughfare through Bend; Bond Street, running parallel to Wall but one block east, was notoriously the rough part of town, offering up saloons, gambling and brothels. Bond Street was disreputable enough that children and "ladies didn't walk…past all those saloons," a situation that lasted well into the 1950s and '60s.)

The population had swelled to 850 by 1910, and by 1911, it was estimated at 1,500; by that time, there were twelve saloons.

Ads in the *Bend Bulletin* for establishments such as the Minnesota Buffet, the White House, G.W. Whitsett's Saloon, The Silvertooth and Hugh O'Kane's The Office promised "Wines, Liquors and Cigars" and often specified a selection of popular whiskies. Olympia Beer was apparently a popular staple as well; The Office advertised, "Olympia beer for sale to families at The Office saloon. Three bottles for $1." Ads for The Silvertooth prominently featured Budweiser Beer, as well as Weinhard's (out of Portland, Oregon). A photo of the interior of the Log Cabin Saloon (on the corner of Bond Street and Oregon Avenue) from the period reveals a sign for Miller High Life. It is certainly possible that one or more saloons also sold beer from the Prineville Brewery, although after 1906, this would have been unavailable.

The growing town clearly had an appetite for beer, which makes one wonder: why was there no brewery established in Bend or, for that matter, elsewhere in Central Oregon? Surely it would seem that such a venture would be successful, and we have already seen how common it was for breweries to spring up on the frontier. Unfortunately, without direct evidence either way, the best we can do is speculate about why.

One strong possible factor is prohibition. This will be covered in more depth in the next chapter, but from 1908 through 1910, Crook County voted under the "local option" rule to go "dry." Bend had been incorporated for only three years, and although it grew rapidly during those three years, local prohibition would have been a death knell for any startup brewery. (The agricultural communities of Redmond and Madras, incorporated in 1910 and 1911, respectively, were even less likely to have a local brewery—although they were not wanting for saloons!) And although the county voted itself "wet" again by a narrow margin in 1910, Oregon as a state enacted prohibition in 1916, four years ahead of the nation.

Another probable factor was simply that the business of opening new, local breweries was on the decline since its peak in the late 1870s. Consolidation by the regional and national brands, better transportation and distribution and the growing temperance movement all contributed to this downturn in the brewery business. Beer was as popular as ever, but when it was available at likely a cheaper cost than the startup and overhead costs of running a brewery on the frontier, shrewd economics must have prevailed.

Finally, geography possibly played a role as well. Despite its growth, Bend was still an isolated community forty miles from the county seat and one hundred miles from the nearest railroad endpoint in Shaniko. Travel to the town—particularly if hauling goods and materials—meant traveling by rail first to The Dalles and then on to Shaniko, followed by the arduous journey over rutted trails that could scarcely be called "roads" or, perhaps even more problematic, from the west over the Cascade Mountains. Perhaps the cost and effort required to import the raw materials needed to build and operate a brewery were considered to be too great? If that were the case, the population may have been content to simply import the finished product.

Still, there are tantalizing clues that brewing beer was on the minds of at least a few locals. Alexander Drake grew hops on his property, and in September 1905, homesteading newcomer Henry Hedges announced his plans to plant a substantial acreage of them on his homestead two miles east of Bend. According to the *Bend Bulletin*:

> *Henry Hedges is preparing a dozen acres of his homestead for a crop of hops next year. A man from the Yakima country was in last week to buy a tract of ditch land near Bend for hops. He said there was no reason why this region should not be as famous a hop producer as the Yakima valley. A.M. Drake has a very thrifty specimen of hops in his yard this season, as has also Mr. Hedges, and he, too, will probably put out a considerable acreage in hops.*

Later in the month, the *Bulletin* noted, "Henry Hedges brought in this week a specimen of the hops ripened on his vines. They are large and full of lupuline and as heavy as first year hops ever are." And the following May, the paper reported that "hop vines show a growth of three and a half feet so far this season."

After years of rumors, anticipation, false starts and rivalries, the railroad finally came to Bend in 1911. This proved to be a pivotal moment in the history of the town and Central Oregon—the rails bypassed Prineville entirely, and suddenly the "upstart" town on the edge of the frontier became the most important one, economically, in the region. Packtrains and horse-drawn wagons were still the primary transport into and out of Bend for many, but the railroad connected Bend to the outside world and provided the means to export the vast wealth of resources that lay at the town's doorstep: timber.

The railroad was two-way, of course, and the year 1911 also saw the beginning of a short-lived era in desert homesteading, as the railroad brought increasing numbers of settlers interested in getting plots of the government land. Homesteading was not new in Central Oregon; the Homestead Law of 1862 allowed U.S. citizens 160 acres of public-domain land provided they could live on it for five years, develop and cultivate it and pay a small fee. "Up to 1890," wrote Raymond Hatton in *High Desert of Central Oregon*, "homesteading in Oregon was essentially confined to the more attractive, fertile, watered lands west of the Cascades." The homesteads of Central Oregon were similarly located near settlements and water sources. However, there were millions of acres of High Desert available, all of it public land—much of it open range used by the stockmen and sheepherders, across which range wars and conflicts still raged—and a revised homestead act of 1909 increased the acreage provided to settlers to 320. With the arrival of the railroad and the subsequent opening up of Central Oregon to the outside world, attention centered on this vast swath of public land, and over the course of the next several years, many homesteads and communities sprung up on the desert.

This homesteading era would not last more than five years, and by World War I, it was virtually over. The reason? Despite the optimism and determination of the settlers to start their new lives, the reality of life on the desert soon dashed those dreams. Lack of resources (particularly water), unforgiving climate, isolation and desolation all contributed to the general failure of the desert homestead. It might be a romantic notion to imagine starting a new life on a big plot of land, growing your own food and livestock and hewing much of what you need by hand—perhaps even brewing your own rustic beer with ingredients harvested and collected yourself. But the reality for Central Oregon homesteaders was much different. They were required to eke out a hardscrabble life in a one- or two-room shack on a plot of waterless desert land. Their attempts to grow rye and other grains were constantly thwarted by jackrabbits, harsh nights and the short growing season. If they were fortunate enough to own a plot of land with enough native bunch grass, perhaps they could even raise a few cows—assuming the coyotes didn't get them.

For those homesteaders who persisted on through the years of Prohibition, many did end up producing their own alcohol—as moonshiners. As noted by the Offbeat Oregon website, "A two-dollar investment in sugar and yeast could pay the bills for a couple months"—ironically proving far more lucrative than dry farming the desert ever could.

The end of the homesteading era and the arrival of the big mills in 1916 effectively marks the end of the frontier era in Bend's history. The transition of the city into a mill and timber town had begun, and it would ultimately become the largest and most important in the region. Prineville, bypassed by the railroad in 1911, recognized that lack of access to the rails would mean certain decline for the town and built its own city railroad in 1918 that connected to the main railroad trunk nineteen miles north and west. However, Prineville still remained largely a quiet rangeland town until the mid-1930s, when the arrival of two big sawmills revitalized its economy, and it, too, became a mill town.

Other Central Oregon towns were going through transitions of their own around this time. Redmond, to the north of Bend, had been settled as early as 1905 and established as an "irrigation town" on the desert fed by the irrigation canal line from the Deschutes River (originating in Bend). The town incorporated in 1910, and in 1911, the railroad arrived on its march toward Bend; Redmond enjoyed slow but steady growth as it developed into the agricultural heart of the region, becoming "one of the largest single bodies of irrigable land in the Northwest." The town of Madras, farther north, was founded as a trade center and town for the surrounding ranches and farms of northwestern Crook County. The town was incorporated in 1910, and when Jefferson County was formed out of Crook in 1914, Madras became the county seat in 1917 following a legal battle over the issue with the nearby town of Culver.

The town of La Pine, thirty miles south of Bend, sprung up in 1910 and was platted and mapped partly in anticipation of the arrival of the railroad from Bend and partly to take advantage of a twenty-eight-thousand-acre irrigation project centered on the area. The establishment of La Pine marked the death of Rosland, a nearby homesteading community that had had an established post office since 1897. (Despite the area's growth, it would be nearly a century before La Pine incorporated as a city in 2007.) And fifty miles north, the town of Sisters, one of the oldest settlements in Central Oregon and the "eastern gateway to two major Oregon Cascades passes" (Santiam Pass and McKenzie Pass), was beginning its transition from a ranching community that was once a major thoroughfare for stock traffic being driven to the summer ranges to a lumber town taking advantage of the extensive tracts of pine forest it abutted.

Despite all of these developments taking place across Central Oregon, one of the greatest changes yet was about to grip first Oregon and then the nation: Prohibition.

CHAPTER 2

PROHIBITION ON
THE HIGH DESERT

J ust before 3:00 a.m. on Monday, March 8, 1926, a terrific explosion rocked the Congress apartments, located at the corner of Bend's Congress Street and Hood Place, southwest of downtown. The apartment building was demolished, and several nearby houses were damaged; none of the residents of the apartments was killed or seriously injured, although in a neighboring home, Alice Bush was buried in falling debris as she slept. Another home, owned by the Mansfield family, had a piece of timber punch through the wall. "Had it continued its line of flight," the *Bend Bulletin* reported, "Miss Mansfield would have probably been seriously injured."

The cause? Dynamite. The targets? State prohibition officers A.F. "Buck" Mariott and C.C. McBride, who had been involved in the shooting death of suspected moonshiner Vayle Taylor the month before. Mariott and his wife were sleeping in their apartment at the time of the explosion and luckily escaped unscathed—due largely to the apparent fact that the would-be assassin was too unfamiliar with demolition techniques to properly plant the explosives to accomplish his or her goal.

Although this was the most spectacular local story occurring during (and because of) Prohibition, it was far from the only one. Central Oregon during Oregon's prohibition years of 1916 through 1933 became, in the words of writer Finn J.D. John, "Oregon's liquor cabinet." The Oregon Outback, as the High Desert region of Central and Eastern Oregon is sometimes called, was a major source of bootleg whiskey and moonshine for the entire state—and beyond. "[Few] parts of the Pacific Northwest," wrote journalist

Moonshine stills like these were common on the High Desert during Prohibition. *Courtesy Deschutes County Historical Society.*

and historian Phil Brogan, "had more moonshine stills in operation…than Central Oregon." Historian David Braly phrased it more directly: "Central Oregon became the moonshine capital of the Pacific Northwest."

To understand how it got to that point, some background is in order. The American temperance movement traces its roots to the 1820s, when the young nation, awash in alcohol, reached "a moment of national doubt and self-reflection," as author Maureen Ogle described it, after a half century of rambunctious independence and excessive economic self-indulgence. "[A]s if awakening from a bad hangover, millions of Americans turned their gaze on themselves and each other, and cringed at the sight." As a result, America engaged in a national reform movement that sought to correct every conceivable societal ill, with alcohol being chief among them.

The state of Oregon, like many states and communities prior to the onset of national Prohibition in 1920, was no stranger to the temperance movement. Temperance took hold in the Oregon country even before the state entered the Union in 1859: in 1844, the Provisional Government of the Oregon territory (not to be confused with the organized incorporated Territory of Oregon, which was established in 1848) passed a prohibition law that was to prevent "the introduction, distillation, or sale of ardent spirits" in Oregon. ("Ardent spirits" referred to beverages in which the alcohol content is measured by proof instead of by percentage.)

It levied fines against violators that were steep for the economy of the period: anyone caught importing ardent spirits into the Oregon territory with the intent to sell would be fined $50 for each offense, while anyone simply caught in the act of selling would be fined $20. If a person were caught distilling spirits, he or she could receive a fine of $100 if convicted. Practicing physicians, however, were exempt and could sell alcohol for medicinal purposes (not to exceed one gallon at a time).

Although this law did not last for more than a few years, the temperance movement was not yet finished in Oregon. In 1854, a prohibition petition was circulated and signed by seventy-four people to ban liquor (the "worm of the still"), but as the idea of prohibition did not enjoy the support of the population of the Oregon territory, the petition was denied.

This first temperance crusade in America from which these Oregon examples are culled lasted from the 1820s through the 1850s, with two strong factors eventually curtailing it: the rise of "non-intoxicating" lager beer that supplanted hard liquor and the Civil War. Those factors, and the undeniable fact that where prohibition was attempted in large cities, rising crime and outright violence in the form of riots convinced most Americans that moderation, not prohibition, was the key to temperance.

Although muted somewhat, the temperance movement never went away, and many Americans genuinely believed that drink—particularly the hard stuff—was a threat. The movement reorganized and gained strength during the latter half of the nineteenth century, with the establishment of the political Prohibition Party in 1869 and, most importantly, the establishment of the Woman's Christian Temperance Union (WCTU) in 1874 and the Anti-Saloon League in 1893.

The WCTU is best known for the welding together of the Prohibition cause with that of women's suffrage, although its members also agitated for a number of other reforms, all intended to improve the lives of others, including prison reform, free kindergartens, vocational schools, eight-hour workdays, government ownership of utilities, vegetarianism, cremation and less restrictive women's clothing. Its rapid growth in membership every decade through the 1930s—decade-to-decade numbers average out to more than 220 percent growth over fifty years—illuminates the role that women played in the temperance movement, with good reason. Women were too often the victims of the excesses wrought by alcohol—more specifically, by the taverns and saloons that provided it to their husbands and fathers. Daniel Okrent, in *Last Call*, painted a vivid picture:

> *A drunken husband and father was a sufficient cause for pain, but many rural and small-town women also had to endure the associated ravage born of the early saloon: the wallet emptied into the bottle; the job lost or the farmwork left undone; and, most pitilessly, a scourge that would later in the century be identified by physicians as "syphilis of the innocent"—venereal disease contracted by the wives of drink-sodden husbands who had found something more than liquor lurking in saloons. Saloons were dark and nasty places, and to the wives of the men inside, they were satanic.*

Without the political standing that the right to vote would provide, women were by and large powerless to do anything about alcohol and the saloon problem. The timing was right: the American public was becoming fed up with the saloons, many of which were dens of prostitution and gambling at worst and community nuisances at best.

The saloons of Central Oregon were no exception. In Bend, the notorious establishments on Bond Street illustrated these points all too well; the town and particularly Bond Street were running "wide open," offering liquor, gambling and prostitution in abundance. Despite the town's growth and development, it was still a very rough and wild era, and the "saloon problem" came to a head in 1912 with the shooting death of Carrie Patterson in a "rooming house" above the Meyers and Wilkey saloon. Anti-gambling and prohibitionist forces seized on this to pressure the city council to clean up the town, and the situation drew the notice of the Crook County sheriff and, soon, Oregon governor Oswald West, who had little tolerance for towns running "wide open." (Governor West had just cleaned up the town of Redmond, having the town's mayor and local marshal arrested while they were playing in an illegal poker game. They subsequently resigned.) Bend made the effort to clean itself up, limiting the number of saloons from twelve down to five with a license fee of $1,200 per year. George Palmer Putnam, then mayor of Bend, later recalled:

> *A reasonable thorough house-cleaning was had. We presented a shining face to the outer world, though perhaps the back of the civic neck hadn't been scrubbed too thoroughly. Mostly the dubious ladies went. What gambling remained became orderly and unobtrusive. The saloons found wisdom in keeping strict hours and discouraging drunkenness. Rough stuff was*

frowned upon. Toughs who wanted to fight were beaten up and sent on their way.

The saloons were also a danger to the town in another way: fire. An anecdote from the book *The River Flows as the Mountains Watch* recounts:

> *There was also the big fire on Bond Street before Prohibition. Just about every business on Bond Street was a saloon or honky tonk. The frame structures were like torches and that whole block of saloons burned to the ground. The men panicked because they were afraid the whiskey would be lost. They rushed into the buildings to get the liquor. Everyone was hustling to keep the hooch safe. They did a pretty good job the first few trips. The trouble was the men kept tipping the bottles to fortify themselves. After several trips, they got a little too tipsy to take the mission seriously. They had a swell time trying though.*

In Madras, the WCTU was well represented by homesteader Rachel Ellis, who even served as Oregon state president for the organization for a time. Ellis was very active in the church, and she was by many accounts an "able and well-informed speaker," imprinting on the memory of many for her speeches about the evils of alcohol. The book *Echoes from Old Crook County* notes, "Among the legion's activities was parading through the 14 saloons on the west side of 5th Street in Madras, where they sang temperance songs and collected money for the WCTU and church."

As important as the role of the WCTU was in the anti-saloon movement and the larger temperance rhetoric, it was the Anti-Saloon League (ASL) that would be instrumental in bringing about national Prohibition in 1920. The ASL was founded in 1893 by Howard Hyde Russell and wielded adeptly by Wayne Wheeler—so adeptly, in fact, that by the 1920s Wheeler was widely recognized as the most powerful man in America, with unprecedented influence over the government. The foundation on which the ASL was organized was ingenious and elegant in its simplicity: it was a campaign not *for* prohibition but rather *against* the saloon. Under this single-minded focus was born perhaps the most effective single-issue interest group the nation has ever known, one that would not only influence and bring about local and national Prohibition but also hold sway over national politics and fundamentally redefine the role of the federal government.

But that would be in the future. In 1887, the WCTU and the national Prohibition Party managed to get a strict prohibition measure on the Oregon state ballot for the election of that year. Oregonians weren't having any of it, defeating the measure by a three-to-one margin. This and other state- and national-level setbacks helped the WCTU, ASL and other temperance organizations to realize that attacking alcohol at the state (and higher) level was fruitless—focus at the local level instead was the key.

Thus were born the "local option" laws, which quickly became the most powerful weapon in the temperance movement's arsenal. Local option allowed for the individual counties in a state to hold elections to determine whether they would remain "wet" or go "dry," allowing the prohibitionists to focus their efforts on a county-by-county basis and, later, under the "home rule" laws, on a city-by-city basis. It was far easier for the temperance movement to ban alcohol in a single county or municipality than an entire state, allowing the drys to chip away at a wet state one city or county at a time.

In 1904, the WCTU and ASL were successful in getting a local option bill passed in Oregon and began working on getting the individual counties to go dry. They were effective, and as one would expect, local option and home rule led to a confusing, convoluted situation in which wet counties bordered dry counties; within a dry county, a city might be wet. If you couldn't buy alcohol in one county, you could simply visit the neighboring county to do so. In Lane County, which was dry, the city of Eugene was also dry, but the city of Springfield was wet. Not surprisingly, Springfield became a popular destination for Eugene residents interested in drinking.

Crook County elected to go dry in 1908 in a two-to-one vote that surprised many residents, wets and drys alike. Crook County at the time encompassed all of Central Oregon: Prineville, Bend, Redmond, Sisters, Madras and more. (Looking at a modern map, the Crook County of 1908 encompassed all of present-day Crook, Deschutes and Jefferson Counties.) Local prohibition was in force as of June 30, 1908, and all of the saloons in the county were forced to look for other, legal avenues of business or close their doors.

Many that survived this period did so by selling soft drinks, cigars and near beer. Others closed. Of course, there were the illegal avenues as well; Dr. Urling Coe, onetime mayor of Bend, noted that the local prohibition "proved to be very wet in spots."

However, by 1910, many residents had had enough of the dry spell, and petitions were filed "by the liquor people" for a new vote on Crook County's local option measure for the fall election. In November, the county (and the state) voted itself wet again, as did nearly all of the cities under the home rule measure—all but Warm Springs, which voted to remain dry.

In Bend, part of the reasoning behind voting the town wet again was the anticipation of the coming of the railroad, as well as the influx of single men they expected to arrive with it. It was a logical move: the licensing of saloon properties was lucrative for the city, which early on earned a majority of its funds from the saloons (one of the first city ordinances passed when Bend incorporated in 1905 was a $600 saloon license fee—high for the time). More single men meant more drinkers, which meant more city revenue. Even so, the saloons and the rough nature of Bond Street were still a problem, and in 1911, the city decided to limit the number of saloons to twelve, with an $800 license fee per saloon, and further restricted the sale of hard liquor so that it could not be sold away from Bond Street except with meals. (The $800 fee was reduced to $300 later that year.)

Throughout it all, the specter of prohibition loomed at both the local and national levels. During the early years of the twentieth century, the Anti-Saloon League had been hard at work on its crusade, through the advancement of local option, its well-oiled propaganda machine, stacking the political deck with drys in governmental positions across the country and capitalizing on America's disenfranchisement with the saloons. A number of states had already elected to go dry and enacted local prohibition ahead of the national movement. In 1913, the ratification of the Sixteenth Amendment, establishing the federal income tax, removed a major roadblock from the prohibitionists' path: the dependence of the federal government on the money generated by alcohol taxes. Many brewers and distillers had complacently assumed that because of the vast budgetary line item their industry generated for the government, the prohibition movement could not possibly succeed. The federal income tax effectively negated this assumption.

The year before in Oregon, a major roadblock to state prohibition was removed: the state granted women the right to vote, seven years ahead of the Nineteenth Amendment granting the vote on the national level. With women having the vote, prohibitionists renewed their efforts in Oregon, and in 1914, a state prohibition measure was once again placed on the ballot.

Unlike the prohibition attempt in 1887, however, the measure of 1914 provoked a bitter fight between the prohibitionists and the wets (backed by the brewers and the liquor industry), and considerable amounts of money were spent on both sides to support their respective causes. Drys enlisted famed preacher Billy Sunday (the Billy Graham of his day) to extol the virtues of life without spirituous beverages; wets brought in famous lawyer Clarence Darrow to speak on free choice and reasonable laws. In the end, it was the pivotal role of Oregon's enfranchised women that carried state prohibition—an estimated three out of every four women who voted chose prohibition—and the law went into effect on January 1, 1916. Oregon became a bone-dry state.

The movement for national prohibition proceeded under the aegis of the Anti-Saloon League, which had successfully stacked the legislative deck of the government with drys. When the resolution for a constitutional amendment was introduced and passed by both the House of Representatives and the Senate in December 1917, anti-German sentiment (and thus, in large part, anti-brewer sentiment) during World War I helped speed its ratification journey through the state legislatures (three-quarters of which were required to enact it). Not to mention the fact that the state legislatures were rigged, as Daniel Okrent termed it, by legislative malapportionment: electoral districts with vast differences in populations being otherwise represented equally in their legislatures. (Gerrymandering is an example of deliberate malapportionment.) Rural districts, which strongly leaned dry, had equal votes in the ratification issue, even though they had far fewer individual voters than the urban districts (which were by and large wet); thus, a state that might otherwise have voted against ratification strictly based on population instead went the other way due to a minority of voters that controlled the majority of districts.

On January 16, 1919, Nebraska became the thirty-sixth state to ratify the Eighteenth Amendment, and it officially took effect on January 17, 1920.

Overall, the arrival of national Prohibition had little impact on Oregon, largely due to the fact that the state's moonshiners and bootleggers already had nearly four years' head start. In Central Oregon, the moonshiners initially kept it local. From Brogan:

The Central Oregon moonshining industry began…when men with little or no knowledge of liquor-making fashioned crude stills from copper boilers and coils, then launched their great experiment with sugar, corn meal, barley, and wheat. At first the potent product from the desert stills was sold in nearby towns to a select trade. Later, as competition increased, the market expanded, and moonshine runners took their liquor into Portland and Seattle. Some of this liquor produced in caves of the High Desert bore Canadian labels.

The High Desert was full of ideal hiding places for the moonshiners' stills: the openings of lava caves, abandoned homestead shacks, sheltered coves and gullies—all spread out over hundreds of square miles. "Every

Law enforcement was busy during Prohibition. Here, a confiscated still operation is on display. *Courtesy Deschutes County Historical Society.*

night," according to Braly, "the countryside…would light up with the fires of whiskey stills."

Law enforcement officials, not surprisingly, were unable to keep up with the sheer number of moonshiners over the vast expanse of land. Part of the problem was that they were too well known; knowing that the local sheriff had headed east into the desert, or detecting him coming from a distance over the wide-open landscape, the moonshiner had plenty of time to vacate his still and evade capture. Newspaper stories from the time read as comical as often as serious, and even sensational, in detailing the law's efforts to enforce Prohibition. On January 16, 1919, the *Bulletin* noted:

> *Bay Rum Popular with the Thirsty*
> *Much Hair Tonic Being Used as Substitute for Whiskey Believes Chief of Police*
> *If bay rum would actually cause hair to sprout, many a human alimentary canal in Bend would be lined with a luxuriant hirsute growth. This is the believe of Chief of Police L.A.W. Nixon, who bases his opinion on the number of empty hair tonic bottles he has found in various places about the city and on the fact that cranial baldness here is not decreasing in the least.*

The February 6, 1919 *Bulletin* added:

> *Whiskey Runner's Car Taken When Bullet Punctures Tire*
> A daring attempt to run liquor into Bend was frustrated late last night by
> Sheriff S.E. Roberts and Chief of Police L.A.W. Nixon, who intercepted a
> cargo of whiskey, eight cases in all, on the LaPine road. The auto carrying
> the liquor stopped only after it had cast a wheel, the tire of which had been
> punctured by a shot from Chief Nixon's revolver.

The April 17, 1922 *Bulletin* reported:

> *Denies Sale of Moonshine*
> Hidden behind trees bordering Drake Road, waiting to intercept a consignment
> of liquor which he had been informed would pass shortly, Police Chief
> Willard Houston was thrown off the scent by a booze sale which took place
> within a few feet of where he was standing, he reported yesterday after his
> arrest Saturday night of Jack Milliron on a charge of selling, and of C.A.
> Mansfield for possessing a quart of moonshine whiskey.

The November 6, 1923 *Bulletin* noted:

> *Varied Brands of Moonshine Are Destroyed*
> Approximately 46 gallons of liquor of various hues and odors, all of it
> confiscated by the Bend police in recent months, was destroyed in about
> an hour Monday afternoon by Chief of Police Peter Hanson and Officer
> Millard Triplett. That was not quite all of the liquor the police had on
> hand, as they kept some for use in the radiator of the police car.

The March 15, 1930 *Bulletin* reported:

> *Thirsty Soil Given Drink of Moonshine*
> One hundred and thirty gallons of intoxicating liquor, including 37
> imperial quarts of "Canadian stuff" which officers say was bottled in
> Bend, poured into the gravel at the rear of the city offices on Bond street
> late Friday afternoon and flowed into the ground through numerous rivulets.
> The "pouring bee" took place under the direction of Chief of Police P.A.
> Thomas, who was carrying out a destruction order issued by Municipal
> Judge G.C. Morgan.

Finally, the August 28, 1933 *Bulletin* noted:

> *Still Explosion Sets Fire Here*
> *One of the most complicated moonshine plants ever seized by Deschutes county officers was taken this morning at 1469 East Third street near Norton avenue. The plant was discovered when the pressure tank exploded, resulting in a call for the Bend fire department.*

And of course, there was the case of the attempted dynamiting of prohibition officers Mariott and McBride in 1926, detailed at the beginning of this chapter. By this stage of the Prohibition era, it had become apparent that the well-known local law officers were unable to curb the moonshining and bootlegging; thus, state officers, unhindered by the same constraints, took over much of the effort. The incident that led to the death of Vayle Taylor (and the subsequent bombing) took place in mid-February at a moonshine plant in the Bear Butte Hills on the edge of the High Desert.

The two officers and a third man discovered the plant in a small gully screened by juniper trees; it was inside a small dugout with a single door, with a large batch (ten barrels) of mash brewing. They hid inside the dugout to await the return of the plant's operator and waited for eighteen hours until Taylor approached the plant the next morning, leading a packhorse. Spying the officers' tracks, he grabbed a twelve-foot-long plank and placed it against the door of the dugout to blockade it, and then he made a circuit around the dugout and an adjoining shed, possibly to look for other signs of intruders.

It was never clear whether Taylor was the operator of the still or, in fact, had anything to do with it at all; though he was rumored to have been involved in moonshining, no hard evidence had apparently ever been found implicating him. At any rate, after his circuit of the plant, Taylor approached the blocked door of the dugout, lit a match and stuck his hand through the window to attempt to see inside. McBride grabbed his hand and shouted that he was under arrest, and Taylor wrenched his hand loose and tried to reinforce the door. McBride and Mariott, guns drawn, broke down the door, and in the process, McBride's gun discharged, striking Taylor in the neck and killing him instantly.

The coroner's jury at the inquest exonerated McBride of the shooting, but feelings ran high in the desert country against the officers; they received a number of veiled threats to their lives, McBride's in particular. McBride, in fact, was the intended target of the bombing. A reward of $750 was offered

Even law enforcement seemed to be surrendering against the tide of illegal moonshining during Prohibition. *Courtesy Deschutes County Historical Society.*

by the county for the dynamiters, but no one was ever charged, and the crime remained unsolved.

Despite the lucrative nature of moonshining, not everyone turned to distilling for their alcohol. The homebrewing of beer thrived during this time as well, particularly for home and personal consumption, as it was the cheapest and easiest method to produce alcohol. The Volstead Act, the legislation enacted to carry out and enforce the Eighteenth Amendment, did not prohibit the sale of ingredients used in producing alcohol, and the breweries—those that survived, at any rate—took to selling cans of malt extract syrup. Add water and yeast, wait a period of time and the syrup fermented into beer. The breweries were generally coy about the obvious purpose behind the sales of the syrups—they could be used in baking, for instance—and Anheuser-Busch was no exception, selling its own brand of hop-flavored malt syrup. The cans of malt syrup were carried by grocery stores, easily obtainable, and "malt shops" blossomed, precursors to today's homebrew supply shops, selling the malt syrups, as well as yeast, bottles and bottle stoppers, filters and more.

It was tougher for law enforcement to catch a homebrewer in the act of brewing than it was to track down a still; in most cases, the beer was

Prohibition-era ad for Budweiser Hop Flavored Barley Malt Syrup. *Courtesy Anheuser-Busch.*

discovered and confiscated after the fact, when it was discovered at all. The brewers were often clever in their hiding places (farmers would hide their beer in the irrigation ditches; one individual hid the beer in a cave he dug under his woodshed, with the opening covered by a pile of wood), although as often as not the beer was simply seized from their homes. And as with the moonshine reporting, stories of illicit beer were often tinged with sensationalism and were borderline ludicrous, as in this story from the November 6, 1923 *Bulletin*:

From VARIED BRANDS OF MOONSHINE ARE DESTROYED
[There] *still remained 47 quart bottles and 27 pint bottles of liquid labelled* [sic] *as beer, which it was not deemed safe to open, because of the well known propensity of that commodity to effervesce.*

Loading three sacks and two boxes full of [beer] *bottles in the police car, Hanson and his two witnesses started a perilous journey to a point outside the city limits. Perilous, because the jolting of the car might have caused a disastrous explosion, but luckily none of the bottles were broken until the journey was ended, at a rocky point where huge boulders stood near the edge of the road….Nearly every bottle, as it broke, showered explosive liquid and bits of glass in all directions. One bottle neck was blown back, narrowly missing the chief's head and nearly piercing the top of the car.*

Then there was this, from the September 12, 1925 *Bulletin*:

WIFE NEEDED BEER, HE HAD TOO MUCH
Too much devotion to his wife caused Louis Skjersaa to pay a fine of $150 in Acting Recorder R.H. Fox's court today.

A local physician prescribed beer as a cure for an ailment from which Mrs. Skjersaa was suffering shortly after the birth of a child.

Skjersaa, in the enthusiasm of his husbandly affection, made a considerable quantity of beer—just how much at one time is not known but when Chief of Police Peter J. Hanson raided the Skjersaa home last night, he found 500 bottles of it there.

Finally, in a note from the September 19, 1925 *Bulletin*:

MORE USES FOR CONFISCATED HOMEBREW SUGGESTED
Two further suggestions, both of them meritorious, were made today as to the proper disposition of confiscated home brewed beer, following Chief P.J. Hanson's announcement that some of it would be tried on a vegetable garden as a fertilizer—the idea being that the various ingredients would be beneficial and the alcoholic part would stimulate growth.

One of the plans advanced today by a dairying expert who happened to be in town was that the contraband beer should be poured over onsilage and fed to dairy cows, or used to moisten bran which would be eaten by the same animals.

By the late 1920s, most Americans had become fed up with the effects that Prohibition had wrought on the country: violent crime had risen dramatically, corruption among law enforcement and the upper class was rampant and enforcement was an ineffectual farce. Alcohol that was confiscated was only a bare fraction of what was trafficked, and much of the confiscated alcohol ended up in the homes of crooked politicians or similarly well-connected individuals. If one wanted a drink, it was easy to find—assuming it wasn't toxic brew laced with chemicals and rank inexperience. It was clear that Prohibition was a failure from the beginning.

With the stock market crash of 1929 and the onset of the Great Depression, the economic impact was reconsidered as well—surely being able to collect taxes on the manufacture of alcohol once again would provide a much-needed boost to the dismal economy. Americans were ready for a change and, in 1932, elected Democrat Franklin D. Roosevelt, who ran on a wet platform advocating repeal of the Eighteenth Amendment. Congress was ready for a change as well, and wheels were set in motion to begin the process of repealing the maligned amendment—no small matter considering many thought that a constitutional amendment, once ratified, was immutable. Add to that the influence of the ASL, which, although it had waned since Wayne Wheeler's death in 1927, was still widely thought to have enough sway over the state legislatures to block the ratification of a repeal amendment.

However, ratification of an amendment by a state legislature is not the only path to ratification, although up until 1933 (and since then as well), it has been the only method by which a constitutional amendment has been ratified. Article V of the Constitution provides that an amendment may be ratified by a state convention rather than by state legislature, three-fourths of the states being required to enact the amendment in either case. Thus, when Congress passed the Twenty-first Amendment, it directed that ratification be enacted by convention rather than by the temperance-influenced state legislatures—the first and only time a constitutional amendment has been ratified in this way.

Congress put forward the Twenty-first Amendment in February 1933, but it would still take time for the ratification process, so in the interim, an immediate solution sponsored by New York representative Thomas Cullen and Mississippi senator Pat Harrison proposed legalizing the manufacture and sale of beer with an alcohol content of 3.2 percent by weight (4.0 percent by volume). The Cullen-Harrison Act was enacted by Congress on March 21, 1933, and signed into law by President Roosevelt on April 7.

Meanwhile, ratification sped through the state conventions. Oregon was the seventeenth state to ratify the Twenty-first Amendment on August 7, 1933, and on December 5, Utah became the thirty-sixth and final state needed to ratify the amendment. Prohibition was finally over.

CHAPTER 3

TIMBER TOWN

THE BOOM YEARS

The year 1916 was a transitional one for the city of Bend, one that would alter the landscape of Central Oregon for years to come. Statewide prohibition came to Oregon on January 1. Deschutes County, the thirty-sixth and final county to be established in the state of Oregon, was carved out of the western portion of Crook County; Bend became the county seat. Two of America's largest pine-manufacturing companies established sawmills on the edge of town, across from each other on the Deschutes River.

The coming of the Brooks-Scanlon and Shevlin-Hixon sawmills was a watershed moment for the city's economy, transforming the town from a raw, frontier agricultural community dependent on irrigation into a mill town, with timber sustaining the region for more than half a century.

Bend was established at the edge of a vast swath of yellow (ponderosa) pine wilderness that had long attracted midwestern timber interests, whose own stands of pine were running short. No wonder: original estimates placed the amount of available timber at some 16 *billion* board feet—to put that into context, it was enough lumber to provide for the framing of 1 million 2,400-square-foot homes. Even at a combined peak between the two large sawmills of cutting about 500 million board feet of pine per year (which they hit in the late 1920s), those estimates would provide for thirty-two years of continuous supply to the mills. And thanks to two world wars and rapid nationwide growth (notwithstanding the Great Depression of the 1930s), lumber was in high demand, and Bend was the town for it.

The Brooks-Scanlon mill, with Pilot Butte in the background. *Courtesy Deschutes County Historical Society.*

The big mills would not arrive until after the railroad had reached Bend, but eastern interests had been aware of and had been scouting the timbered area for more than a decade previously. As early as 1898, M.J. Scanlon of the Brooks-Scanlon Corporation had visited the pinelands and selected holdings of land that the company later acquired. Then, in about 1904, a renewed interest in the Timber and Stone Act of 1878 (which sold 160-acre blocks of timberland that was "unfit for farming" to individuals for $2.50 per acre, provided they pledged to not transfer the title) led to a rush of land fraud cases in Oregon by which hundreds of thousands of acres of timberland acquired by individuals were later acquired by the corporations. The government put an end to this in 1905 by withdrawing the forest reserves from the public domain and subsequently created the national forests.

In May 1915, the Shevlin-Hixon Corporation of Minnesota announced plans to build its sawmill in Bend, on the west side of the Deschutes River across from the old Farewell Bend Ranch. And in August of that same year, Brooks-Scanlon announced *its* plans to build its sawmill on the east bank of the Deschutes River, directly across from Shevlin-Hixon (and on the old Farewell Bend Ranch). Both mills were complete and in operation by the spring of 1916.

The population grew accordingly. From 1910 to 1920, the town saw a population increase of more than 600 percent, growing from an estimated 850 in 1910 to 5,414 in 1920. The population surged again during the '20s to reach 8,821 by 1930. Many of the newcomers were single men, looking for work in the mills or in one of their many logging camps; others came in from the desert, abandoning their hardscrabble lives on the dry homesteads to take jobs in the mills to support their families.

To source their timber, the sawmills established railroad logging camps, outposts in the deep woods populated by the lumberjacks and timber men who located and felled the trees, limbed them and transported the logs to the railroad to be delivered to the mills. When a camp moved, the rails for the trains moved with it. It was not uncommon for a logging camp to be located in a single location for a year or more, with many loggers' families joining them in the camps; they became self-sufficient, self-contained communities in their own right, hosting schools, company stores and more. The "bungalows" and other buildings were designed around a railroad car. "Once trees in one location had been cut," noted one anthropological study, "the entire camp was loaded aboard railroad flatcars and transported to the next area of logging activities." The largest of Shevlin-Hixon's camps, aptly named "Shevlin," contained three hundred to six hundred residents in the "town" and had many of the amenities one would expect in a real town, including a tavern with pool tables and slot machines.

While alcohol was never tolerated on the job in the camps, it was present during the off-hours—though, of course, a tavern was not the norm in the logging camps. Being self-sufficient, it was far more likely that one would find homemade wine and beer instead, and often the brewing duties fell to the women who ran the household. A first-person account from *The River Flows as the Mountains Watch* tells the story:

> *We'd cook the old-fashioned way, stews and soups, sauerkraut. We made beer and made homemade wine. That beer has that thick foam from the barley and it was good stuff. It didn't last us very long. The guys would play and drink, you know. Us girls kept washin' bottles and getting ready for another batch. We'd put the boiler on the stove and fill it with water and then we'd make the beer in that. Then we'd put it behind the stove to ferment for 2, 3 days. When the yeast'd foam up it was ready. We kept it cold in the root cellar before we got refrigerators.*

Interestingly, the start of Bend's timber town boom coincides with the start of prohibition—first Oregon's statewide prohibition in 1916 and then the national version in 1920. As such, there is no clear picture of how Bend's beer attitudes were affected by the growth of the mills until after 1933, although Prohibition itself provided sensational stories and glimpses. Working in the sawmills was hot, noisy, dusty, sweaty labor, and the growing population of single men, working long shifts, was thirsty for beer to wash the sawdust out of their throats. During Prohibition, many of them almost certainly spent some of their paychecks on the bootleg alcohol or brewed and/or distilled it themselves. At one of the Shevlin-Hixon logging camps during that time, there was a camp cook operating a small still on the back burner of a cookhouse stove; as the camps considered good cooks to be among the most important employees, the still was tolerated as long as the meals kept coming.

When Prohibition was repealed, Bend's beer scene unsurprisingly mirrors that of the rest of the nation: the beer started flowing again, and there was no shortage of business for the newly opened (or reopened) taverns and bars. With the millworkers in town, Bond Street was once again the center of it all and doing lively business. Over the next few decades, the rough-and-tumble nature of a blue-collar mill town, combined with the large number of single men, reinforced the "wide open" reputation of Bond Street that it had enjoyed during its frontier heyday, avoided by women and children traveling alone.

Another oral reminiscence from *The River Flows as the Mountains Watch* notes:

> *There were a lot of beer places in Bend in '48. Down there on Minnesota Avenue they had beer places everywhere. Because of the mills there were lots of single men in town. Over there where Eddie's Canton is now* [former Cantonese restaurant, now a barbershop and salon], *there used to be a big enormous rooming house with a lot of rooms and stuff. Then where the Eagles is* [formerly on the corner of Greenwood Avenue and Hill Street], *they had these places, where they…you know. We're talking about them red light houses. When the railroad fellars would come into town they'd stay overnight or something. Bond Street was the place with most of the beer places and those other kind of houses.*

Some places were more respectable than others, at least on the surface. For instance, the Palace, "Bend's Recreation Center," had been established in the O'Kane building in 1923 as a gambling and gaming hall. Following Prohibition,

Ad for the Palace tavern, appearing in the *Bulletin*, early 1940s. *Author's collection.*

Interior of the Gateway Tavern, which was located near the mills. *Courtesy Deschutes County Historical Society.*

it naturally added beer and wine to the menu (at least, legally) following its renovation in 1935. Ads from the '30s declared, "When better beer is made, [proprietor] Harold Kline will serve it!" and advertised Rheinlander, Schlitz, Blitz-Weinhard, Alt Heidelberg and Acme Beer. The Palace was a "favorite haunt of Bend businessmen" and retirees, and letters to the editor in the *Bend Bulletin* in 1973 and '74 lamented a change of ownership that replaced "the heart of Bend" with a "frenetic big city tavern."

Some of the taverns were naturally preferred by different nationalities of residents and thus became favored gathering spots for those groups. The D and D Club, for example, was a favorite of the Irish community in Bend. The D and D was run by John Daly and his brother, themselves Irish immigrants (John Daly was naturalized in 1939), and it is still in existence today, marking it as one of Bend's longest continuously running businesses (along with the Pine Tavern restaurant).

Throughout it all, the beer in Bend mirrored that of the rest of the nation following Prohibition and World War II: the consolidation and growth of the mega-breweries, which brewed lighter and more homogenous lagers in response to the changes of a modern America, influenced by post-repeal alcohol laws; the development of the interstate highway system; the rising number of televisions per household; a national palate that preferred blander, processed foods; and an overall decline in the beer market. The beers became lighter and plainer; the biggest breweries poured money into national advertising and distribution, often pushing out smaller regional breweries from supermarket shelves (the "supermarket" itself was a recent development, proliferating in the years following the Second World War). Consumers gravitated toward the big brand, the familiar beer, convinced that it should be light, pale, dry and best drunk ice cold.

It didn't help that for all its failure, Prohibition was successful in one respect: Americans drank less, despite the years of absurd proliferation of illegal alcohol. "[An] entire generation of men and women," wrote Maureen Ogle, "had not tasted alcohol for decades—or ever—and had no plans to do so." The breweries that had survived Prohibition stumbled into this new reality and others—Americans by and large now preferred to drink their beer at home rather than at the taverns, leading to a trend that would see packaged beer (as opposed to draft) accounting for 80 percent of the market by 1960. As a result, many smaller breweries simply couldn't keep up with the cost of doing business when that cost included expensive packaging lines and the development of a distribution network to support that packaging. Many of these smaller and regional breweries turned to mergers and consolidation just to survive, just as the national giants were doing, and as a result, the industry was steadily downsizing.

In a move that might seem eerie in its similarity to what was happening in the brewing industry at the time, Brooks-Scanlon purchased the Shevlin-Hixon plant and all its timber holdings in 1950; the Shevlin-Hixon sawmill closed in December of that year. The timber business had been booming since the end of the Great Depression, which had a direct impact on the timber supply, and by the middle of the century, the two directors of the mills realized that with the remaining timber reserves (Shevlin-Hixon estimated a mere three years' supply remained in its holdings), one mill could last much longer than the two.

The rapid growth that the mills had brought to Bend in 1916 had shaped the city into its distinctive east/west sensibility, with Shevlin-Hixon employees tending to live on the west side of the Deschutes River and Brooks-Scanlon employees on the east side (matching the placement of the mills themselves). The millworkers lived in bungalows that had been quickly erected to meet the growing population influx, while the business and professional families generally chose houses clustered around Drake Park near the river (on both banks).

The loss of the Shevlin-Hixon payroll was keenly felt in Bend for several years, but the lumber industry soldiered on, with Brooks-Scanlon modernizing its plant in 1958 and other lumber-related companies establishing new jobs for the area, such as Willamette Industries' KorPine particle board plant, established in 1966 in a partnership with Brooks-Scanlon. But other developments were taking shape that had been quietly percolating for years. "Bend definitely continued as a mill city," wrote Brogan, "but it was making a strong bid for a new source of income as a recreation area that was gaining wide recognition."

The city and region were becoming known for another type of industry: tourism.

CHAPTER 4

RECREATION AND TOURISM

From the beginning, Central Oregon has been well regarded for its recreational possibilities, its quality of life and its "healthful, invigorating climate"; a *Bend Bulletin* editorial from August 1903, ruminating on the town's railroad prospects beyond what timber might bring, suggested that "the cultivation of a popular health resort" would "undoubtedly bring the railroad" to Bend. And in a July 1912 special section, the *Bulletin* further waxed rhapsodic on the region:

> *The western portion of Central Oregon is a land of rare beauty—of varied attractions far greater than any but the initiated realize. Indeed, for out of door recreation, for variety of scenic interest and for healthfulness, no territory in all the Northwest surpasses the country that lies along the Deschutes River and flanks the Cascade Mountains on their eastern slopes.*
>
> *In this great region there lies a veritable paradise for out of door lovers and people who would make homes where there is recreation, health and happiness as well as the prosperity of dollars and cents. The investor, the business man and the farmer are not the only ones for whom Central Oregon has interest. The tourist, sportsman, camper, automobiler and health seeker will all find reward in this big, new land.*

In his book on the history of Central Oregon, *East of the Cascades*, Phil Brogan wrote:

*Recreation possibilities of the Deschutes Country were known to the early-
day settlers. After harvest each season, it was the practice of many ranch
families to pack food and bedding in farm wagons and drive to favored spots
in the high country, to camp, fish, hunt, and gather berries. But those early
seekers of forest recreation were a mere trickle compared with the great rush
to the woods that followed the second world war.*

Among the recreational opportunities the region afforded were camping,
hiking, hunting, fishing (the rivers were so full of trout that a daily catch limit
in the early part of the century was set at 125 per person—a number that
seems almost ludicrous today), canoeing and mountain climbing. Other scenic
attractions that drew visitors included lava caves (particularly the ice caves,
which generate ice year round), the lava beds south and west of Bend, the
mountain lakes of the Cascades and the Paulina Mountains to the southeast.
Bend was on the southerly route to Crater Lake for visitors from Portland and
the Willamette Valley, which drew thousands of visitors each year.

Skiing and other winter activities developed with the arrival of lumber and
millworkers of Scandinavian descent in the 1920s and '30s; they were among
the first to ski the backcountry and the slopes of the Cascade Mountains,
having grown up skiing in the snowy winters of Minnesota or the Old Country
from which they came. The Skyliners Club was formed in the 1920s by a group
of Nordic skiers to assist in search and rescue operations in the mountains, as
well as to promote the sport of skiing in the region. In 1936, the club built and
opened the Skyliners Lodge on Tumalo Creek, about ten miles west of Bend,
and it became a popular winter destination for skiers until the Mount Bachelor
Resort was developed and opened in 1958.

Successful from the start, the driving force behind the development
of the ski resort on Mount Bachelor was one man, Bill Healy, who ran a
family-owned furniture store in Bend. Mount Bachelor (the "mountain"
designation technically did not come about until 1983; until then, it was
officially "Bachelor Butte") grew to become one of the most successful
ski resorts in the nation, offering world-class skiing (the U.S. Olympic Ski
Team began training at Bachelor in the mid-1960s) and technology ahead
of others in its high-speed lift systems and computerized ticketing systems.
Skiing filled the tourism gap in the area (between the end of hunting season
in the fall and the start of fishing season in the spring) and grew to be one of
the most important tourist industries; a study in 1962 revealed that out-of-
town winter visitors brought in $500,000 to the local economy, and in 1980,
a similar study found skiers responsible for 80 percent of the winter lodging

Bohemian beer truck. *Courtesy Deschutes County Historical Society.*

business, with the Bachelor resort accounting for 20 percent of the tourism business in Deschutes County. It would be fair to state that although Bend and Central Oregon enjoyed recreational tourism prior to the 1960s, tourism as a major economic driver for the region truly began with the opening of the Mount Bachelor Resort.

An interesting side note about Bill Healy's son, Cameron: he worked at the ski resort until he left for the University of Oregon in Eugene in the mid-1960s, after which he took up yoga and Sikhism and changed his name to Nirbhao Singh Khalsa. He started a natural food distribution company in Salem in the 1970s that evolved into food manufacturing and eventually into Kettle Foods (as the company was renamed in 1988), whose signature product was Kettle Chips. Nirbhao then partnered with his son, Spoon Khalsa (Bill Healy's grandson), to open Kona Brewing in Hawaii in 1994.

Development of the other resorts to capture more of the tourist and lifestyle trade followed Mount Bachelor, beginning in 1965 with the announcement of Sunriver Resort, to be built on the former site of Camp Abbot, which was a U.S. Army training ground during World War II. The Inn of the Seventh Mountain, catering heavily to the Mount Bachelor winter recreation seekers, was announced in 1967 and opened by 1969. Black Butte Ranch, west of the town of Sisters on the road to the Santiam Pass, with sweeping vistas of the Cascade Mountains, was started in 1970.

Mount Bachelor, as seen from Crux Fermentation Project in the Old Mill District. *Author's collection.*

Although Bend, like the rest of the country, experienced the trends of consolidation and homogenization of beer after Prohibition and the Second World War, there are still indicators that people were thinking of beer with the same sensibilities that they approached life in Central Oregon—premium beer to match the region's exceptional lifestyle. Ads for the Palace highlighted "better beer" (as mentioned in the previous chapter). Witness also an ad on page three of the June 2, 1938 edition of the *Bulletin* for Hop Gold Pale Export lager, taking up 40 percent of the page: "NEW KIND OF BEER FOR BEND!" screams the masthead in larger type than even the *Bulletin*'s own; ad copy extols its "3 FULL MONTHS AGING!" and quotes brewmaster Ed Schwind as stating that it's "the finest beer ever offered to the West."

Of course, a certain amount of hyperbole is always to be expected in advertising. But they do reveal hints and trends in how beer is perceived regionally. It's also important to note that during this time the national breweries, led by Anheuser-Busch and Schlitz, engaged in coordinated, nationwide advertising campaigns, spending enormous amounts of money advertising on television (accounting for an astounding 84 percent of network television revenues in 1952!), in magazines and newspapers and on billboards. The regionals, unable to compete in the national arena, relied heavily on localized print advertising, tailoring their message to (what they believed to be) the local tastes.

As such, ads targeting the outdoor recreation that Bend had to offer must have resonated, particularly as the tourist industry grew. Ads for Washington's Olympia Brewing in the *Bulletin* provide a glimpse into that evolution. Ads in the 1930s following Prohibition were fairly minimal, focusing on Olympia's feature quality ("It's the water") and, betraying not-too-far-removed-from-Prohibition sensibilities, highlighting "[b]eer, the light refreshment beverage of millions of temperate people." The 1940s opted for a more information-rich approach, focusing on quality over quantity (explaining why the beer could be brewed only at Tumwater, "It's the water," again), emphasis on the brewery's historic roots and a nod to "America's Original Light Table Beer" (a patriotic touch that surely didn't hurt during the war years). By the '50s, the shift toward a recreational, lifestyle-choice attitude had emerged, opting for less information and more imagery, such as enjoying a round of beer after golf, during a barn dance or as an après-ski beverage after hitting the slopes. It was "Olympia…with pleasure!" This trend continued into the next decade, with a focus on packaging and portability—particularly oriented toward convenience in accompanying outdoor recreation. (In a curious bit of coincidence, Olympia's Tumwater, Washington brewery was also built on the Deschutes River—a fifty-mile river that empties into Puget Sound.)

Portland's Blitz-Weinhard Company follows a similar trajectory in the local ads, with a reliance on its recognition among Oregon consumers, its quality and its history (the oldest continually operating brewery in the Northwest). "Is your husband a pantry snoop?" asks one ad from 1938 ("And you will be, too, if you keep frosty bottles…in your refrigerator"); another from 1945 compares the beer to a Stradivarius violin. By the late '40s and early '50s, the company was highlighting its "new taste in beer" ("light and lively"), revealing the increasing national trend toward lighter lagers. By the 1960s, the outdoor, recreational angle was in full swing; images such as fly-fishing a lake in the shadow of a snowy mountain and a lakeside picnic with mountains that resemble the Cascades in the background are paired with the portability and convenience of taking Weinhard beer along on such excursions.

Although not an advertisement, but just as revealing, a 1958 editorial in the *Bulletin* reveals the ingenuity toward which Blitz-Weinhard approached its advertising as public relations (as well as the editorial writer's admiration for the brewery in its efforts):

Blitz-Weinhard beer ad, appearing in the *Bulletin* in the 1950s. *Author's collection.*

The Blitz-Weinhard company announced…that it would send free to anyone outside of the state who requests it a Douglas-fir seedling.

The offer is being made, according to [C.P. "Cork"] *Mobley* [public relations manager for the Blitz-Weinhard], *to let the other 99 per cent of the nation's population see how the favored few in Oregon live. A tree will be sent, in the company's words, to any "who are unfortunate enough to live outside of Oregon." All the company wants is a name and address.*

In the late 1960s, Blitz-Weinhard was distributed in Central Oregon by Neel Distributing, whose ads zeroed in on the local lifestyle: "We're lucky to live in Central Oregon," one ad proclaims. "Anytime is 'fun season' in Central Oregon," states another. In 1970, Neel Distributing reportedly sold 52 percent of all the beer sold in Central Oregon, thanks to the Blitz-Weinhard account.

By the 1970s, despite the inroads made by Big Beer (at that time made up of Anheuser-Busch, Schlitz and Miller) and the dwindling regional breweries, Oregon overall and Central Oregon in particular continued to be fiercely independent, favoring the "local" breweries like Blitz-Weinhard and Olympia, which owned 32.5 percent and 23.2 percent of the Oregon beer market in 1970, respectively. (The two brewers had jockeyed over the top spot over the past several decades; in 1960, Olympia had 28.1 percent of Oregon's sales compared to Blitz-Weinhard's 20.5 percent.)

During this time, there was a movement growing in America that would have a direct impact on beer. Americans were beginning to reject the establishment, distrusting large corporations and the government, a sea change that was informed by the counterculture movement of the 1960s, as well as factors such as the Vietnam war, crushing recession and Watergate. This rejection naturally extended into food and drink as well, and many instead flocked to local, artisanal, flavorful foods and complex, characterful drinks like wine and coffee in lieu of bland, heavily processed foods filled with chemicals and preservatives.

So, too, were Americans rediscovering a world of beer beyond the borders of pale/light/lager America: those who had served in the military overseas, as well as tourists (especially in Europe), were exposed to styles of beer quite unlike anything available at home. Returning home, unable to find the same character in their beer, many turned to import beers—the import and premium beer market soared during the 1970s, rising 88 percent in the first half of the decade. Of course, many of those same imports were not much better than what they found at home, and more were degraded by poor handling and storage—no matter, since choosing an import was a lifestyle choice, the same rejection of the establishment that characterized the period.

Still others looked beyond imports and chose an alternate path that meshed further with the small, artisanal movement: brewing their own beer at home. Homebrewing had, of course, thrived during Prohibition, and even though it was illegal (*especially* so), "malt shops" selling hopped malt, yeast, bottles and other supplies thrived. The 1970s saw a curious parallel to Prohibition in regards to homebrewing: it was still illegal (thanks to a poorly worded statute legalizing home winemaking after repeal), and homebrew shops proliferated (usually as supplemental to suppliers of home winemaking).

Homebrewing was a quiet affair, secretive in its illegality, but it was growing rapidly. Homebrew clubs traded information and techniques. Books were self-published (such as Portland author Fred Eckhardt's *A Treatise on Lager Beer* in 1969 and Byron Burch's *Quality Brewing: A Guidebook for the Home Production of Fine Beers*). It had become so common and mainstream that the government finally legalized it in 1978, with President Jimmy Carter signing it into law in October.

There was certainly homebrewing going on in Central Oregon prior to 1978, although until it was legalized that year, there was no real way to gauge just how prevalent it was. A subsequent editorial in the *Bulletin* in February 1979, titled "Home Brew," is prescient of the rise of the craft beer industry in the state:

> *The relaxation of federal regulations could bring about a renaissance in home vinting and brewing in Oregon…With increasing concern over additives in beers, hops—once a common Willamette Valley crop—could make a comeback. Who can imagine a better combination than local malts and pure Oregon water brewed up into a keg of mountain fresh draught in the privacy of your own kitchen?*

Over the following years, the region would develop a vibrant homebrewing culture. The Bend Park and Recreation District offered a class on brewing at home not long after it became legal. The newspaper ran occasional articles on local homebrewers and home beer making in general. In 1983, the City of Redmond added a homebrew beer and amateur winemaking competition to its annual Oktoberfest celebration. And by 1985, Don Boller, owner of Don's Wines in downtown Bend, was offering brewing supplies for sale at his wine shop, estimating that they accounted for 20 percent of his sales. Although Boller apparently had stopped carrying supplies by 1991, a dedicated homebrew supply shop opened in Bend in 1992 (and has been in existence, first as the Home Brewer and then as the Brew Shop, ever since).

Tourism continued to grow in Central Oregon throughout the 1970s, becoming the region's second-most-important industry behind wood products. Bend's own attitudes toward the tourist industry were changing as well as the industry grew. Despite the region's history of attracting visitors and the growth of winter recreation and the resorts, Bend was still largely a blue-collar mill town that enjoyed its isolation. Residents moved there for the quality of life the area afforded, hoping to find a quiet, remote mountain community. But by 1979, the first signs of the recession that would characterize the early 1980s were noticed, with Brooks-Scanlon Inc. acknowledging the "moderate recession" and reporting a 33 percent drop in earnings from the year before. That recession of the early '80s would prove crippling to the local lumber and wood products industry, the ramifications of which would linger on in Bend for longer than much of the rest of the country largely due to the region's historic dependence on wood products.

Tourism was less affected, and in 1983, despite having seen a decrease in visitors the year before due to both the recession and poor weather, tourism and recreation knocked lumber out of the top economic spot, bringing $225 million to Deschutes County (followed by wood products at $205 million and agriculture at $16 million). The tourist industry wasn't a remedy for the recession—Central Oregon was plagued with skyrocketing unemployment, and downtown Bend was marred with high vacancy rates and boarded-up businesses—but in supplanting the timber industry, it set a viable course for the region's future.

It would prove to be a difficult transition that would last the better part of a decade, and by 1994, it could be said that the era of timber had finally come to an end with the closing of the Brooks-Scanlon mill. By the late 1990s, in a final symbolic supplanting of timber by tourism, the former mill properties were redeveloped as a mixed-use shopping and dining district, aptly known as the Old Mill District, with a large outdoor riverfront amphitheater, parks, trails, art galleries and more.

Despite the recession, Oregon was enjoying a brewing renaissance during the 1980s, with a small but growing number of humble craft breweries—dubbed "microbreweries" due to their vastly diminutive size and production output compared to the giants of the industry—springing up first in Portland and then slowly around the rest of the state. By 1988, the renaissance had come to Bend.

CHAPTER 5

LAYING FOUNDATIONS

DESCHUTES BREWERY AND OTHER PIONEERS

Downtown Bend, Monday, June 27, 1988: Deschutes Brewery opened its doors to the public at four o'clock in the afternoon. Owner and restaurateur Gary Fish had moved to Bend a mere seven months earlier after scouring Northern California for the ideal location to open his brewpub and had landed in Bend in the fall of 1987 with the intent to "create a lifestyle business."

The timing was right. Only two years before, Oregon had passed into law bill SB 813, the "Brewpub Bill," legalizing on-premise sales of beer from a brewery directly to customers, thus paving the way for the establishment of the restaurant-microbrewery. This was a crucial turning point for the nascent brewing industry in Oregon; prior to the passage of the Brewpub Bill, not being able to offer beer directly to customers had forced the few fledgling craft breweries into the production-and-distribution model to sell their beer. This gave them two options: they could self-distribute directly to taverns (so long as they did not own or have an interest in the establishment), or they were required to sell their beer to distributors under Oregon's three-tier system. The distributors then sold the beer to retailers. However, the national beer brands had a virtual monopoly on the distribution system, making it all but impossible for the small brewers to get carried by a distributor focused on selling a particular corporation's brands.

By early 1985, there were only two microbreweries operating in Oregon, both in Portland: Columbia River Brewing (which would be renamed "BridgePort" as the popularity of its eponymous beer and later brewpub

Deschutes Brewery taps and a pitcher of beer. *Courtesy Deschutes Brewery.*

grew), and Widmer Brothers Brewing. These, like the short-lived Cartwright Brewing, which lasted from 1980 until only late 1981, were strictly small-scale production breweries, cobbled together with scavenged and refurbished equipment to produce kegs of beer destined for self-distribution. Recognizing that the ability to be able to serve their beer on-premise directly to customers would be a crucial element to their success, and inspired by the examples of California and Washington in pioneering brewpub legislation, Columbia River's Dick and Nancy Ponzi; brewer Karl Ockert; and the Widmer brothers, Kurt and Rob, joined forces with Mike and Brian McMenamin (of the McMenamins pub chain), along with Art Larrance, Fred Bowman and Jim Goodwin (who were planning to open their own brewpub, Portland Brewing), in an effort to get the law changed.

The first version of the bill, HB 2284, was introduced to the Oregon House in January 1985 and subsequently flew through the House with no resistance. The Senate was another story; the bill stalled and was tabled in April largely due to two reasons: resistance to the idea of allowing Coors to retail its beer in Oregon (which had absolutely nothing to do with the original bill but was seized on nonetheless as a reason to oppose it) and political pressure from distributors who didn't like the idea of breweries selling their beer directly. By late May, the distributor resistance had softened, but the Coors issue was still looming; a revised bill that had combined the brewpub and the Coors legislation, SB 45, was once again killed by the Senate.

However, the brewpub language had been inserted by House representative Verner Anderson into bill SB 813, which dealt with liquor licensing for bed-and-breakfasts. Without the Coors association, SB 813 passed quickly and without opposition, and the Brewpub Bill passed on June 17 and was signed into law by the governor on July 13. (Ultimately, Coors did find its way to Oregon shelves shortly thereafter. The crux of the argument preventing Coors from entering Oregon's retail market stemmed from a 1937 state law prohibiting unpasteurized beers from being sold in containers of less than one gallon in stores. In fact, Coors had been selling its kegged beers in taverns and restaurants. In 1984, Coors came to Central Oregon's taps by way of Bachelor Beverage Company, which was co-owned by Brad Wales, who would more than two decades later become a partner-owner in Bend's 10 Barrel Brewing Company.)

The passage of the Brewpub Bill in July paved the way for the brewery public house, and subsequently the McMenamin brothers established Oregon's first post-Prohibition brewpub in the fall of 1985 at their Hillsdale Pub in southwest Portland. Columbia River followed suit in the spring of 1986 with its own Bridgeport Brewpub, and Portland Brewing opened its pub immediately afterward.

The McMenamin brothers had already been building their own unique chain of pubs and taverns and approached beer a bit differently than the other fledgling breweries. While they loved beer and supported as many of the new breweries as possible with taps at their many establishments, they weren't particularly interested in distributing their own beer beyond their own pubs, opting instead to build their brand by offering specialty beers that could (for the most part) be found only at one of their many properties. After establishing their first brewery at the Hillsdale Pub, they followed up the next year by establishing the Cornelius Pass Roadhouse in Hillsboro in May and in July opened up the Lighthouse Brewpub in Lincoln City (to become the first post-Prohibition brewery on the Oregon coast). Over the next two years, they launched the Fulton Pub and Brewery in Portland (May 1988), the Highland Pub and Brewery in Gresham (June 1988) and the High Street

Brewery and Café in Eugene (November 1988), establishing a total of six breweries of their own in the state by the end of 1988.

Elsewhere in Oregon, brewpubs were popping up in what must have seemed like unlikely places, considering that Portland was widely understood to be the epicenter of the craft brewing renaissance: Hood River Brewing (later to become Full Sail) opened in the town of Hood River in 1987; Corvallis's first microbrewery, Oregon Trail Brewery, opened in July 1987; and perhaps the unlikeliest of all, Roger's Zoo opened up in the coastal town of North Bend in January 1987 (the brewery portion later closed in 1993).

So, by the fall of 1987, Oregon's craft brewing scene was promising, if nascent. Gary Fish, then located in Salt Lake City, Utah, had been watching the growth of the microbrewery movement with interest and likened the growth in the industry to that of the wine industry two decades before—an industry with which he was very familiar, as Fish's family was growing wine grapes in California during the late 1960s and early '70s and thus were a part of the state's modern wine renaissance. In addition to getting in on the ground floor of a growing movement, Fish, a fifteen-year veteran of the restaurant industry (starting out as a dishwasher at age sixteen and working his way through college waiting tables before moving on to restaurant management), saw another appeal, as related in a recorded interview:

> *My dad and I started talking; and as opposed to Utah, in California where a brewpub was legal, you could be the manufacturer* and *the retailer—eliminate the middle man. My dad was used to a model where you plant grapevines; it's a minimum of five years until they're producing. You make wine, you put it in a bottle for two years, ship it to a wholesaler, give them sixty- or ninety-day terms…to the model of a brewpub where basically you get paid in cash thirty days after you lay in your raw materials. It's kind of like, "Wait a minute!"*

Getting into brewing made sense. Running it as a restaurant made sense. The next steps were to learn about the brewing side of the business and to find the perfect location to open a brewpub. Although based in Salt Lake City, where he had attended college and continued working in the restaurant industry afterward, Northern California was the lure initially. Fish sold his share in the restaurant in Salt Lake City in which he was involved and moved back to Berkeley, California, with his parents in July 1987 to work for Ed Brown ("basically for free," said Fish), who was launching Rubicon Brewing in Sacramento at the time. The experience proved invaluable in learning the brewing side of the brewpub equation; at the same time, he was crisscrossing Northern California, seeking an ideal location to open a brewpub of his own.

However, the California market at that time was not particularly conducive to starting up a new brewery business. Skyrocketing real estate prices, breweries already in planning or development and building moratoriums were all contributing to the frustration of the search. And then Fish's parents, who were born and raised in Oregon, had recently returned from a college reunion in Corvallis and had passed through Bend to visit friends—and couldn't stop talking about it. Intrigued and worn down by the California hunt, Fish decided to check out the town, visiting in September '87.

The stars seemed to line up, with a number of factors contributing to the draw of Bend as the location for the new brewpub. First, Bend was hit hard by the early 1980s recession, which lingered in the area for longer than in many places elsewhere in the country; at the same time, the lumber industry—which had for so long sustained the regional economy—was collapsing, and the town was midwifing the difficult transition from lumber to a primarily tourism- and recreation-based economy. As a result, there was a lot of commercial space available downtown, and real estate was affordable—particularly attractive considering the inflated prices that Fish was repeatedly encountering in California. Understandably, the city was very supportive of the idea of developing any new project that could help stimulate the local economy and fostered a receptive and inviting business climate.

Then there was the lifestyle factor. Despite the down economy, the region's recreational opportunities were drawing the tourists and visitors who could help provide a reasonably steady source of income—drawn to Bend in the winter by the Mount Bachelor ski resort and in the summer by the promise of beautiful weather ("three hundred days of sunshine a year" was one popular boast) and an abundance of summertime activities. For all that, Bend still only had a population of about seventeen thousand residents, precisely the type of small-town atmosphere that Fish and his wife were seeking to establish the business and raise a family.

The next two months were a whirlwind. In October, Fish brought his wife, who had still been in Salt Lake City, to check out the town, and by November—barely two months after that very first visit—they had moved to Bend in time for Thanksgiving. During those two months of investigation that led to their all-in commitment to Bend, Fish talked to everyone he could about a brewery ("Everyone we met," said Fish, "said, 'Sure you can do that here. I'll be your first customer!'") and had even settled on a location

The Gray, Fancher, Holmes and Hurley law offices building, which would become Deschutes Brewery. *Courtesy Deschutes Brewery.*

in downtown Bend: the former Gray, Fancher, Holmes and Hurley law offices building located at 1044 Northwest Bond Street. (The only other contending space up for consideration was a building on Northeast Third Street—then the main thoroughfare of Highway 97 through town—which now houses a Pizza Hut restaurant.) With the location secured, renovations and development could commence.

Gary Fish wasn't the only person interested in opening a brewery in Bend during that period. At the beginning of 1988, the U.S. Forest Service was looking for someone interested in taking over property management for the historic Skyliners Lodge, located more than ten miles west of Bend. The lodge had been built in the 1930s as part of Bend's first ski area on Tumalo Creek and had been added to the National Register of Historic Places in 1978. The forest service, which had made the lodge available to groups and individuals for recreational use for a number of years, was looking to get out of the property management business and solicited proposals for alternative solutions. Among the four plans submitted was one from Duane Bateman, a local homeowner who lived nearby on Skyliners Road, who proposed a microbrewery.

The forest service rejected the proposal, but the idea of opening a brewery must have stuck in Bateman's mind, for within a few months, he was planning another brewery for Bend, more earnestly this time. He enlisted

Deschutes Brewery Public House under construction in 1988. *Courtesy Deschutes Brewery.*

John Harris (left) with Gary Fish. Harris was Deschutes Brewery's first employee. *Courtesy Deschutes Brewery.*

John Harris, a brewer from McMenamins in Portland, to partner with him and help launch the venture.

Harris had been hired in 1986 to brew at the newly established Hillsdale brewpub, the third brewer hired by McMenamins. Prior to that, he had been homebrewing a bit, mostly using malt extract, and found a similar situation at Hillsdale: the beers were initially being brewed using malt extract, purchased from California by the fifty-gallon drum. Harris also found a homebrewer's sense of experimentation permeating the endeavor, as they tried brewing all sorts of concoctions miles away from other commercial breweries of the day—among the more unorthodox releases the company lists are Blackberry Ale, Mars Bar Ale (using whole candy bars), Java Ale, Spruce Ale and Purple Haze. Mike McMenamin set the tone in 1985 when the brewery opened: "The only rule is there are no rules. The main thing is to have fun!"

Predictably, brewing wildly experimental beers using malt extract under less-than-ideal conditions (small kettles, open fermenters and no temperature control) led to beers that beer writer Vince Cottone in his 1986 *Good Beer Guide* called "weird house brews" that were "a gaggle of gamey and goofy homebrew-style brews."

Brian McMenamin had no illusions about that time. "Oh yeah, we were doing weird stuff, which is what we wanted to do—that's why we did it. We weren't gonna make a Budweiser; we were gonna have our own fun. So we were throwing candy bars in, and we were doing all kinds of crazy stuff. Because people were saying, 'You can't do it,' so we were gonna do it," he shared in an interview. "I remember some of those early beers were *not* good beers." It was the McMenamins' love of beer that drove them forward and allowed brewers like Harris to keep pushing the envelope.

Harris enjoyed the creativity that brewing at McMenamins offered, something he would not have found at one of the other breweries at the time, even as he had reservations about the quality-control issues they encountered with the malt extract and the overall lack of technical control they had over the brewing process. When the Cornelius Pass brewery opened, he went to brew there, and when Hillsdale transitioned from the malt extract to start all-grain brewing, Harris returned so he could enjoy the greater control over the beer that all-grain brewing allowed. During his time at McMenamins, Harris had a hand in the recipe development of now-standard beers, including Hammerhead and Ruby Ale.

Bateman had introduced himself to Harris in 1988 with his Bend brewery idea and hired him to consult on the project. They initially looked at Bend's old mill district as a possible location (years later, that area was formally revitalized as the "Old Mill District," with shopping, a theater, dining and hotels). Harris, realizing the effort and pitfalls involved in starting a brewery, insisted that they attend a two-day UC–Davis brewing class to get an understanding of the undertaking. During that trip, it came out that Bateman didn't have the

John Harris oversees the very first brew (milling grain) at Deschutes Brewery, June 2, 1988. *Courtesy Deschutes Brewery.*

funding for the venture and didn't want to give up control for investment money. Harris, needing a steady paycheck, decided to find another job and applied for the brewer position that Gary Fish was advertising for Deschutes Brewery. He was hired as the brewery's first employee.

During the first half of 1988, the brewery started to take shape. Fish had hired Frank Appleton, who had opened the Horseshoe Bay Brewery in British Columbia, Canada, in 1980 (North America's first post-Prohibition brewpub) as a consultant to help design the brewhouse and develop the recipes for the first three beers (Cascade Golden Ale, Bachelor Bitter and Black Butte Porter). Ed Ripley, of Ripley Stainless, also out of British Columbia, built the ten-barrel brew system. The building was being remodeled as well: originally, there was a small courtyard-type space where the front of the building was offset back from the street; this was removed, as the front of the building was pushed forward to accommodate more seating.

However, when it came time to hire staff, Fish underestimated the kitchen talent that was available. According to Fish in an interview:

We had quite a bit of reporting on us through the Bulletin, *and when it came time to advertise for hiring our initial staff, I was prepared to be completely inundated, and* nobody *showed up. Literally nobody showed up! I figured the bare minimum I had to hire was twelve employees, and at the end of the week I had fifteen applicants. And, I later mused, those fifteen applicants, the reason they applied with me was because they had already worked everywhere else in town.*

This was to presage the following six months after the brewery opened in June of that year—a turbulent, uncertain period during which Fish questioned his decision to open a brewpub in Bend more than once. He now believes that Deschutes was ultimately in the right place at the right time, but it was not an overnight success. The concept of craft beer was still new to the blue-collar town, so people weren't quite sure what to make of the brewpub; many didn't think it would last. The first kitchen manager lasted only two weeks, so Fish assumed that role in addition to his other duties in running the restaurant portion of the business. Business in the depressed town could be slow, so slow that "[y]ou could shoot a gun off in here a lot of nights, and nobody would notice," quipped Fish. There were even nights in which he sent all the employees home and ran the pub himself.

Meanwhile, Harris was busy in the brewhouse, brewing the three core brands and a number of seasonals, which filled the fourth tap slot. (The brewpub at the time had four draft lines on a total of eight tap handles.) The first four seasonals Harris brewed were Wychick Weizen, Mirror Pond Pale Ale, Bond Street Bock and Jubelale. He also continued to tinker with the core recipes, particularly Black Butte Porter; the recipe that Appleton originally devised for the beer was relatively light, more of a brown ale in style (in Harris's estimation), and over the course of the next few batches, he tweaked and revised the recipe to bring more chocolate and dark malts into the mix, until the beer was in line with his idea of what a porter should be. He also instituted what he dubbed "Stout Wednesday," whereupon he would put a keg of a seasonal stout on tap each week.

That winter (dubbed the "Dark Winter of 1988" by Harris), disaster struck: infected batches of beer, one after another. They couldn't figure out the source of the infection, had to dump batch after batch and were down to three tap handles (out of the eight); both Fish and Harris were questioning their decisions.

Finally, Fish brought in Dave Logsdon (founder of Wyeast Laboratories, a dealer of pure brewing yeast cultures, and a founding partner and first brewer of Full Sail Brewing) as a consultant to help troubleshoot the problem. They ended up tearing the whole system and everything else apart to find and remedy the source of the infections. As it turned out, they stemmed both from flaws in the original brewhouse design and from mistakes in the welding—the local welder did not know how to weld stainless steel, which in turn led to bad welds in the piping that were unable to be cleaned properly. With the brewhouse design issues, the placement of the grain mill also caused billowing clouds of grain dust to permeate the inner walls of the brewhouse; the steam subsequently coming out of the mash tun, up the pipe with the flawed welds, got into the walls as well, turning the dust and grain flour into dough—a ripe environment for bacteria and wild yeasts. They tore out the walls, reworked the system, brought in a different welder to re-weld the steel and piping and finally solved the problem.

That first winter of '88 also saw the first bottling of a beer that would become iconic for the brewery: Jubelale, a malty English-style Winter Warmer. They bottled the beer by hand, directly from the taps, in used 750ml champagne bottles that had been salvaged and cleaned. Harris estimated that they bottled thirty to forty cases that first year. The following year, they again bottled Jubelale in champagne bottles, and in 1990, they switched to twenty-two-ounce bottles, which were bottled by a company in Portland that was doing mobile bottling for wine. Jubelale has been bottled every year subsequently, and since 1995, Deschutes has commissioned a new regional artist to design an original work of art to be used for the label.

Aside from Jubelale, the only other beer that was bottled before 1993 (when the brewery's expansion and bottling line were completed) was a special one-year anniversary beer that Harris brewed for June 1989. Harris wanted to brew a hoppy English-style ale and acquired East Kent Goldings hops from the Anchor Brewery in San Francisco. This "Year Beer," as Harris dubbed it, was also hand-bottled from the taps in champagne bottles in a "super small bottling."

With the brewery infection problems solved, Deschutes turned the corner from that first "Dark Winter" into a brighter spring, and business improved. Fish had hired a kitchen manager who understood food, as well as how to run a restaurant kitchen, and the quality of the menu improved almost overnight. The brewpub hosted live music for a short time, which helped bring in customers. Those customers could buy beer to go—bottled in forty-ounce screw-cap bottles filled from the taps (in a precursor to the growlers of today). "Sporty 40 we called them!" laughed Harris. "A six-pack of 40s was a good day!"

The brewery had signed on with Haines Distributing and was able to sell its beer at the Mount Bachelor ski resort. Despite the improvements, however, cash flow was still very poor—they had the beer and the capacity but not the sales. Although the craft beer market was slowly growing, Bend was still "very much a Bud Light kind of town," with only a handful of establishments besides Deschutes selling craft beer (among those few locations were McKenzie's, Player's Grille and Stuft Pizza, all downtown). Portland was an attractive market, leading Oregon's craft beer scene and growing. Harris was good friends with Jim Kennedy, who was with the distributor Admiralty Beverage in Portland. Kennedy called and said that there were tavern owners who had been through Bend, tried Deschutes' beer, really liked it and wanted to put it on tap at their places; however, while the brewery had the beer, it didn't have the kegs.

Kennedy had some old Golden Gate kegs and sold a number to Deschutes, where they filled several and piggybacked them on the back of a Haines Distributing truck full of recycled cardboard on its way to Portland. Suddenly "we were in the wholesale business and we didn't even know it," said Fish.

The popularity of the beer was huge in Portland, and orders compounded after that—from one pallet to two, then four and so on. Sales in the Portland area fueled growth, and Deschutes began scrambling to expand to manage the increased demand. The beer that was proving such a hit was Black Butte Porter. Kennedy had convinced Fish and Harris to lead with the Porter as their flagship beer because it was distinctive from every other craft beer offering at the time—and none of the other breweries was leading with anything like it. The nearest leading beer in similarity was BridgePort Ale, the flagship beer from BridgePort Brewing (née Columbia River), which was a dark ale ("medium reddish-brown," according to Cottone) more akin to a brown ale than a porter.

Deschutes added more tanks, expanded the back wing of the building, added a grain silo on the roof and still grew. The restaurant side of the business was growing as well, becoming busier as the popularity of the pub grew (thanks in no small part to the beer and the improvements to the menu); soon the pub was one of Bend's popular nightlife destinations. It was busy enough that Fish had to hire a doorman for a short while to manage the flow of the crowd. The brewing staff had increased to include brewers Mark Vickery, Tim Gossack and Tony Lawrence, working with Harris, and the beer's popularity was spreading, sparking more local interest in craft beer. Although Fish was adamant that the three core beer brands should be on tap all the time, seasonals like Mirror Pond Pale Ale consistently outsold the core Bachelor Bitter. Obsidian Stout was popular, and Black Butte Porter continued to draw fans to the dark beer. Deschutes beer was pouring at Mount Bachelor, as well as at the Sunriver and Black Butte Ranch resorts, not to mention at markets across Oregon and in Washington. They brewed 310 barrels of beer the first year; by 1991, that number had grown to 3,954.

The brewery rented the building behind them on Harriman Street to use as a warehouse to store and wash kegs. (That building is now known as the "Old Cigar Building," although Fish thinks it should be called the "Old Beer Building.") Semi trucks had to park on the street in front of the warehouse to load the shipments of kegs on their way to Portland and elsewhere, and the city took notice. "We started to get letters from the city about operating an industrial operation in the downtown commercial business district," said Fish. Deschutes had expanded all it could at its downtown location, and demand was only increasing; it was time to plan for more, to begin searching for property to kick off the next wave of expansion. This was early in 1992.

The property they located was on the corner of Colorado Avenue and Simpson Avenue, on 3.75 acres of land that Fish had negotiated with developer Brooks Resources to subdivide, and plans were laid in for an impressive facility: a twelve-thousand-square-foot, three-story building (with an additional level below ground) housing a fifty-barrel production brewery and bottling line.

John Harris would not be present to oversee it, however. After four years in Bend, the town's still-in-progress transition from lumber to tourism was wearing on him, and his wife was not happy there and wanted to move back to Portland. With Deschutes starting to explore its expansion possibilities, Harris didn't want to design the production brewery without the possibility of commissioning it if his future was not going to be in Bend. Thus, he made the difficult decision to leave in the spring of '92. Harris returned to Portland, where he was hired by Full Sail Brewing to run its Portland operation at Riverplace, next to the McCormick & Schmicks's Harborside Restaurant. During his tenure at Full Sail, he was responsible for the brewery's specialty releases and created its Brewmaster Reserve series. Harris brewed at Full Sail for two decades and left in 2012 to start his own venture, Ecliptic Brewing, which opened its doors in October 2013.

After Harris left, roles expanded for Vickery, Gossack and Lawrence, as the brewery sought to expand. Development of the new production brewery and the head brewer role fell to Tim Gossack, who worked with Frank Appleton and equipment manufacturer JV Northwest to design and install the fifty-barrel brewing system for the new facility—the first system of that size and configuration for the ten-year-old manufacturer JVNW.

While Gossack spearheaded the production facility, Mark Vickery ran the brewery at the pub. Vickery had been bartending at BridgePort Brewing (and developing a love for craft beer) in 1988 when he met Harris, and in January 1989, he came to Deschutes to tend bar and work as Harris's assistant brewer.

Tony Lawrence had come to Bend from Lake Tahoe, seeking the snowboarding opportunities offered by Mount Bachelor, and was hired on as a dishwasher for the brewpub's night shift in 1989. He and Harris became friends, and Harris, observing his good work ethic, invited him to work in the brewery washing kegs. He subsequently followed a common path for brewers working their way up in the industry, from keg washing to keg filling and then on to cleaning tanks, mastering the CIP (clean-in-place systems) before becoming the swing shift brewer for the brewpub. When the production brewery came on line in late 1993, Lawrence transferred to it and would earn the bulk of his experience mastering larger-scale brewing.

Fish sent Gossack and Vickery to the Siebel Institute in Chicago in 1992 to further their brewing training, and it was at Siebel that Gossack met Dr. Bill Pengelly, a biologist who had been serving as associate program director of the Cellular Biochemistry Program at the National Science Foundation in Washington, D.C. Pengelly had received his PhD in biology from Princeton University in 1980, moved to Oregon in 1982 and became immersed in homebrewing. "My cell culture laboratory at the Oregon Graduate Institute served my new hobby well," he recalled in an interview published online, "as I was able to efficiently propagate yeast, initiate a yeast library, and sterilize vast quantities of bottles in a single autoclave run." As the hobby progressed along with the Oregon brewing renaissance throughout the 1980s, with a growing number of homebrewers going professional, Pengelly, interested in a similar midlife change, enrolled in Siebel.

Gossack must have been impressed with the knowledge and experience Pengelly had to offer, for he hired him; Pengelly started at the brewpub in 1993. It fell to Lawrence to train Pengelly, and he later recalled:

> We chuckle about it now. Here we have myself, which was pretty much a high school dropout surf bum, and then Dr. Bill Pengelly, PhD, was brought on to the team, and quite honestly he had all the scientific knowledge and was very well-educated, brewing education, everything—biology, chemistry, etc. I had to train him. It was quite the odd couple. It was pretty strange!

Ground had been broken for the new production facility by November 1992.

Deschutes' expansion also heralded a larger awareness and growth of craft beer in the region, one that had been building for more than a decade. The *Bulletin* had added a semi-regular beer column, written by a reporter who was also an avid homebrewer; Bend's first dedicated homebrew supply shop, the Home Brewer, was opened by Scott Woehle in early 1992 (when Don's Wines stopped selling supplies in about 1991, home beer makers had to drive to Eugene or Portland for supplies or purchase them via mail order); and, most tellingly, a number of enterprising individuals, eyeing the popularity and growth of the town's sole brewery, proposed opening microbreweries of their own (although several would not pan out, two did).

In March 1993, the state of Oregon's Highway Division was developing a new parkway for the city of Bend and required the relocation of two railroad depot buildings; it entertained a number of proposals for what to do with the buildings. One of the submitted proposals was for a microbrewery and restaurant, with relocation to Colorado Avenue and Industrial Way near the original Brooks-Scanlon mill site.

In November of that same year, Oregon State University student Eric Stagg filed a land-use application with Deschutes County to develop a brewpub in the Sunriver Business Park, in a portion of the Sunset Realty building. He ran into opposition from the owners of the nearby Sunriver Village Mall over land-use requirements that effectively killed the project.

Back in Bend that same month, businessmen Dave Hill and Jerry Fox were hoping to launch the Brooks Street Brewery downtown, in a building a few doors up from the historic Pine Tavern restaurant overlooking the Deschutes River. Although they "both had experience in drinking beer," Fox recalled, they had no experience in brewing it. Fox credited Hill with the idea to start a brewpub, and despite the need for extensive renovations for the building they purchased, they hoped that the brewery would be open by the following summer.

That timeline proved to be overly optimistic, but the plans for the brewpub were not: the Bend Brewing Company (the name had been changed "in order to give it an identity that would be easy to associate with the city in which it was located," said Fox) opened its doors in 1995, becoming Bend's second craft brewery. However, they were the *third* brewery for Central Oregon overall—the Cascade Lakes Brewing Company, located in the nearby town of Redmond, had beaten them to the punch and opened the year before.

Brothers Steve and Dave Gazeley launched Cascade Lakes Brewing in 1994 on a shoestring budget, piecing together a twenty-barrel brewhouse from salvaged equipment, including used dairy tanks from the nearby Eberhard's Dairy. They located the brewery in a five-thousand-square-foot industrial space just west of the Redmond Airport; unlike Deschutes, they planned to operate strictly as a production brewery, at least at first. The first beers to roll out of the brewery (brewed by the Gazeley brothers themselves) were Rooster Tail Ale and Monkey Face Porter, released in kegs and painted twenty-two-ounce bottles (the same kind of silk-screened labeling that breweries such as Rogue were also utilizing). The twenty-two-ounce bottles were not to last long, for the brothers acquired a 1950s-era Maheen bottling line configured for twelve-ounce bottles.

With the new bottles, a third beer joined the lineup, Angus MacDougal's Dagger & Dirk Scots Ale, which was soon followed by Weissbier. The labels featured colorful, cartoonish artwork, contrasting markedly with the stylistic, distinctive oval logos employed by Deschutes.

Meanwhile, Deschutes Brewery's production brewery was completed and operational by late 1993, in time to bottle that year's edition of its Jubelale on the new bottling line. The next beer off the bottling line in January 1994 was Bachelor Bitter, which would soon be followed by the other core beer, Obsidian Stout (a popular seasonal beer that had joined the year-round lineup by this time). In order to scale up the core recipes that had been developed and calibrated for a ten-barrel brewing system to a fifty-barrel system, it required brewing and testing many batches to achieve the same taste and consistency that consumers were used to from the brewpub. (Former Deschutes brewer Paul Arney noted, "Black Butte Porter took a year of consistent brewing to accomplish it.")

Those weren't the only challenges facing Deschutes with the new brewery. The major challenge the company would face for the next dozen years was the one that prompted the expansion in the first place: growth. "Growth in the industry was something no one could anticipate but we all had to deal with," said Fish. The new production brewery marked the beginning of a time of transition for the company, as it struggled internally with transforming from a restaurant-based business with small-brewpub roots to a major beer manufacturing operation.

Fish's remarks translate easily from the situation faced by the Bend-based brewery to the craft beer industry as a whole. The industry saw a 35 percent growth in 1991 rise over the next few years to 58 percent by 1995. "The exuberance and electricity in the air were palpable," wrote Harry Schuhmacher. "These were heady numbers, and everybody from disenchanted Wall Street financiers to burned-out engineers to young get-

Cascade Lakes Brewing's early label designs. *Author's collection.*

rich-quick swashbucklers was looking longingly at our little industry." In fact, many of those people entered the industry, drawn by the huge growth figures, interested more in capturing some of that market share and making a quick buck than in focusing on brewing quality beer. The earlier generation of brewers, many of whom started out as homebrewers, by and large had entered the industry for the love of the beer, not to make money. It has been said that brewers of that earlier era shared an attitude of, "We'll drink what we want and sell the rest." No wonder: through those first decades of the craft brew era (which many consider to have started in 1976 with the founding of New Albion Brewing in California), craft brewers by and large didn't have to worry about market share, trends and the like; they were exploring territory that had been dark since before Prohibition, pioneering new styles and flavors to generations of American palates used to bland, light lager. It's fair to say that they *were* brewing for themselves as much as for the marketplace.

This dichotomy—brewers concerned with the quality and integrity of their beer versus entrepreneurs interested in the money to be made—characterized the craft brewing industry of the mid- to late 1990s, ultimately resulting in an oversaturation of beer of questionable quality and a shakeout of the marketplace. By 1997, growth had dropped to a mere 1 percent and remained between 0 and 6 percent through 2003.

Deschutes itself would not see a similar drop and continued to expand throughout the '90s; however, rapid, transitional growth can be a struggle for any company, and Deschutes was no exception. It was a similar dichotomy to what was playing out on the national level: the brewers were concerned with maintaining a quality, hands-on process and retaining creative freedoms, yet they were faced with the conundrum of needing to maintain growth and cash flow for the growing company. "Not everyone was inspired by that," said Fish. Ultimately, this change would serve as a catalyst over the next decade for the departure of much of that early era brewing staff (whom Tony Lawrence would characterize as the "Old Guard"), many of whom would move on to other successful brewing ventures large and small.

At the other end of the spectrum, Bend Brewing Company opened to the public in February 1995, located in a building on Brooks Street that had once housed a glassblower. Dave Hill and Jerry Fox oversaw renovations, which included the installation of a seven-barrel brewhouse in the upper level, a cramped space packed with tanks and equipment that looked out a large picture window to the dining room below. The west-facing dining room itself looked out onto the Deschutes River through large windows. The brewer was Scott Saulsbury, an alumnus of Deschutes Brewery who had joined Deschutes in 1993. The brewpub launched with a lineup of five ales: High Desert Hefeweizen, Metolius Golden Ale, Elk Lake IPA, Outback Old Ale and Pinnacle Porter.

Hill ultimately had other interests besides the brewery, and Fox bought him out in that first year of opening and brought in his daughter, Wendi Day, to manage the day-to-day operations of the brewpub. Day had moved to Bend with her family from Cleveland, Ohio, in 1986, and after graduating from Bend High in '88, she left for Arizona State University to study accounting and marketing. It was at Arizona State that she met her future husband, Rob Day, and her post-college years found her in Seattle working in retail management. When the offer came from her father to manage the business, Day and her husband returned to Bend in 1995.

Bend Brewing Company. *Author's collection.*

From the beginning, Bend Brewing focused exclusively on the brewpub and restaurant business, with its small-batch beers served only in-house and not packaged for distribution. The brewpub soon became a popular downtown destination, particularly as a post-recreation stop for locals and tourists alike. "Bend Brewing is more upscale than its friendly competitor, Deschutes Brewing Company," reported *The Brewpub Explorer of the Pacific Northwest*, published in 1996. "Large windows offer a pleasant view of the park and the Deschutes River. Antique tables and chairs possibly once gracing an old English pub are scattered about the main dining and bar area."

By February 1996, the brewing duties for Bend Brewing had been taken over by Dan Pedersen, a graduate of the Siebel Institute who had spent the previous year and half brewing in Eugene, Oregon, for the Eugene City Brewery. Scott Saulsbury moved on to southern Oregon, with brewing stints at Wild River Brewing in Grants Pass, Caldera Brewing in Ashland in 2001 and Southern Oregon Brewing in Medford in 2008.

Over in Redmond, the Gazeley brothers had found that their Cascade Lakes beer was a hit with the locals, so much so that after only a year in business they realized that many wanted more than just to buy six-packs of their beer at the grocery store—they wanted a pub, someplace they could sit down with the beer and have a meal. The Gazeleys listened, and the result was the opening of their Seventh Street Brewhouse in Redmond in 1996, in a 1,300-square-foot home that had been converted into a brewpub that showcased their beers, both the regular lineup and specialties and cask ales that were brewed on the small system they installed. That same year, they also hired their first brewer who was not a brother: Jack Harris.

Harris came to Central Oregon from Boulder, Colorado, where he had been brewing at Mountain Sun Pub and Brewery for the previous three years. But like his namesake, who had helped get Deschutes Brewery off the ground, he had gotten his start in 1990 with McMenamins, brewing at the company's Cornelius Pass Roadhouse and then at its Lighthouse Brewpub in Lincoln City. Harris would remain at Cascade Lakes for only a year, living in the front office of the brewery with his dog, before moving to Cannon Beach on the Oregon coast to brew for Bill's Tavern & Brewhouse, where he would spend nine years before leaving to open Fort George Brewery in Astoria in 2007.

As a backdrop throughout these years of brewery development and growth, Bend was growing as well. The town had finally emerged from the recession of the early '80s late in that decade, with tourism taking the economic lead for the region. The population rose from 17,263 in 1980 to 20,469 in 1990 and then jumped to 52,029 by 2000—a rate of growth more than three times the state's average. A factory outlet mall opened in 1992 offering more than two dozen stores, and Bend was subsequently "discovered" by nationwide retail chains, which opened new stores in the region during the '90s, including Costco, Walmart, Home Depot, Target and others. A six-screen movie theater opened in 1994, the largest theater in the area to date. (The older Tower Theatre, downtown, closed that same year.)

This growth was driven by the influx of a generation of aging Americans who had discovered Bend while looking for a small town in which to retire, as well as a stream of younger Gen Xers and Millennials drawn to the region by a combination of recreation, lifestyle, climate and the relatively cheap cost of living. As a result, the incoming population was a curious mix of retirees, outdoorsy youth, "refugees" from the California real estate market and others seeking the lifestyle and opportunities that Bend had to offer. As the population grew, growth itself became a considerable segment of the local economy, with real estate and construction (much of that, ironically, remnants from the collapsed wood products industry) forming a significant pillar to that growth.

Deschutes had a notable year in 1996, as head brewer Tim Gossack departed for Tempe, Arizona, to open the Rio Salado Brewing Company (purchasing the recently established Seideman Brewing to do so). In his place, Dr. Bill Pengelly took the reins as director of brewing and would guide the brewery through the next seven years of growth. Several other notable brewers joined Deschutes around this time, including Mark Henion, John Van Duzer, Jimmy Seifrit and Paul Arney—all of whom would eventually follow up their tenure at Deschutes with key roles at other Central Oregon breweries in the coming years.

Over the next several years, Deschutes would see its output grow from 3,954 barrels in 1992 to 76,100 barrels in 1998 and 102,000 by 2001 (roughly 30 percent per year). This spurt in production was driven by the demand for its beer around the Pacific Northwest that spurned a seemingly continuous phase of expansion that persisted through the '90s, with approximately 50 percent of its sales coming from Portland and the Willamette Valley and another 20 percent from the Seattle area in Washington. This phase of expansion was finally complete by 1999 and included multiple four-hundred-barrel fermenting and bright tanks, a new German-manufactured Krones bottling line and a new IDD keg line that allowed the brewery to switch from Golden Gate to Sankey kegs. This period also saw the departure of Mark Vickery for Golden Valley Brewery in McMinnville, Oregon. Vickery would remain at Golden Valley until 2013, when he left to open Grain Station Brew Works in McMinnville with his business partner, Kelly McDonald.

Brewing duties at Cascade Lakes in Redmond had transitioned from Jack Harris to Tom Kemph, and they added several additional beers to the bottled lineup, as well as seasonals available at the Seventh Street Brewhouse. Despite their growth—or perhaps because of it—they were still brewing all of the beers on the original used dairy equipment, and over the next few years, the quality would suffer. ("Butterscotch Rooster Tail Ale!" acknowledged current partner Chris Justema in a 2014 interview. "Like having a shot of butterscotch schnapps in your beer.")

Over at Bend Brewing Company, the brewpub continued to be an increasingly popular destination for locals and tourists alike. Brewer Dan Pedersen left in 1998, and brewing duties were taken over by Christian Skovborg, a former brewmaster from the defunct Nor'Wester Brewing. By 2000, Jerry Fox was anxious to retire and wanted to turn over ownership to his daughter, Wendi Day. Day was reluctant at first, but she partnered with her kitchen manager, Terry Standly, to purchase the business from her father.

Homebrewing was continuing to thrive as well, in Bend as well as around the country. Much of the craft brewing movement was driven by homebrewers, as many professional brewers got their start by homebrewing and developing the knowledge and skills to help make the leap to a brewing career. In fact, it would be an enterprising homebrewer who would launch Central Oregon's fourth brewery (and smallest to date) in 2001.

Bend's sole homebrew supply shop, the Home Brewer, had changed hands several times since Scott Woehle opened it in 1992, first to Dan Elsey and then to Elsey's son, Micah, for a year and finally to Larry Johnson in 1997. The shop occupied a small, 250-square-foot space behind a hair salon on the south side of Bend. In 1999, the shop was stagnating: Johnson had been working his full-time job as well during the year and a half that he had owned it, and he had struggled to maintain consistent hours and inventory, as well as reliable employees; as a result, he put the shop up for sale. In the fall of that year (October 1, to be precise), the Home Brewer was bought by Tyler Reichert.

Reichert was a recent transplant to Central Oregon, having arrived in 1998 from Vermont, where he had been working for a nonprofit environmental company, living on a farm in the middle of 3,500 acres of forestland. Because it was off the grid, and since (particularly in winter) there were times when he had to hike in to the farm over a mile and a half with an eight-hundred-vertical-foot climb, Reichert began homebrewing as an alternative to having to carry in heavy cases of beer. When he moved to Bend, he brought his brewing equipment and joined the local homebrew club, of which Johnson was also a member. When Johnson put the Home Brewer up for sale in 1999, Reichert thought that he would be able to devote the time and effort necessary to make the shop successful.

He was and he did. Reichert impressed the local homebrewing community with his knowledge and increased selection of ingredients, and the Christmas season of that year (1999) was incredibly busy, with one of those busy days seeing a line of customers extending outside the door of the tiny shop space. That small footprint and a burglary in the summer of 2000 prompted Reichert to begin searching for a new, larger location. By late summer, he had located a larger space on Division Street and moved.

The new location had enough space that Reichert originally conceived of offering a brew-on-premise operation, where customers would be able to brew their own fifteen-gallon batches of beer on the shop's equipment, ferment it there and take it home with them when it was ready. However, the brew-on-premise market had already become oversaturated and had begun to fizzle out, and Reichert realized that "it was harder to teach people how to make beer than just to give them finished beer." So, he decided to pursue the brewery route instead. He acquired his brewery license in December 2000 and located the equipment of (ironically) a failed brew-on-premise business the following January. It was located on the southern Oregon coast, in the town of Bandon, although after looking it over, he decided that the price was too high for the system and declined. In February, the owner (motivated to make a deal) contacted Reichert and ended up selling the equipment to him at well lower than the asking price.

Reichert and a friend drove to Bandon with an eighteen-foot flatbed trailer behind their truck and spent the better part of a day loading every piece of equipment onto the trailer. The drive back, over the mountain passes in the middle of winter, provided both a hair-raising journey and the name of the future brewery:

> *We left like seven at night, super overloaded, super heavy. And it was in February, and there was a storm the night before, so the roads were super slick. It was crazy. It was like seventeen degrees out over the pass, which was good, even though it made for an icy drive—it was so cold that the truck didn't overheat…We had a full moon rising up in the east. So you're on the west side of the pass, you're in [a] heavily forested [area], which means the highway is like black, dark. Black ice, super cold; it's like, "Man, we do not wanna break down, wreck, anything right now"…just ridiculously white-knuckle. And then once we crested over past Mount Thielsen, started going down, the moon's coming up, and all of a sudden it's bright: you can see the road; you can practically see the stop sign ten miles away.*

Reichert had his name: Silver Moon Brewing. And he had a one-barrel brewing system, with a seven-barrel primary fermenter and a seven-barrel Grundy conditioning tank. Reichert did all the brewing himself from the location on Division Street, initially offering up four beers: Hound's Tooth Amber, Bridge Creek Pilsner, Harvest Moon Heffe and Dark Side Stout. He hired Tyler West in 2002 as an assistant to handle the CIP and learn the brewing system, and production rose gradually from about ninety-seven barrels the first year to about two hundred barrels by 2004. Output was small, particularly compared to a brewery like Deschutes, but the region was receptive to the beer and the idea of a fourth brewery.

While Tyler Reichert was moving the Home Brewer and taking the first steps to start his brewery, another brewing interest that had been eyeing Bend as a location for a brewpub operation found an opportunity: Portland-based McMenamins secured a two-year option to purchase the old St.

Francis Catholic school in downtown Bend in October 2000. In early 2001, it announced plans to renovate the property to turn the campus into a hotel and restaurant, with an on-site brewery, a theater, event spaces, a soaking pool and extra lodging in bungalows at the east end of the property.

The school itself had relocated to a modern, newly constructed campus on the east side of town earlier that year, and the Catholic archbishop had called up McMenamins to offer it the older property. In the years since the McMenamin brothers had helped to launch the brewpub revolution in Oregon, they had become known as the "guys who do old buildings," finding historic properties and converting them into unique destinations often revolving around overnight lodging, dining, music, events and, of course, beer. They had started in 1991 with the Edgefield, a former poor farm that had been built in Troutdale, east of Portland, at the beginning of the twentieth century; on the seventy-four-acre plot of land, they developed a winery, a European-style hotel, restaurants and bars, a spa, a distillery, a concert and event space and more. The Kennedy School in northeast Portland followed, and by the end of the decade, they had cemented their reputation as historic property renovators; many in Bend were eagerly wondering when McMenamins would come to town.

However, it would still be several years before the Old St. Francis School would be open; in early 2002, McMenamins received the go-ahead to move forward with the permit process, and in January 2003, it finally closed on the deal to buy the property, planning to begin development by the fall for a 2004 opening.

During this time, Cascade Lakes Brewing had been in the process of changing hands. The Gazeley brothers sold their brewery in early 2001 to partners Rick Orazetti and Doug Kutella, who were interested in revitalizing the business and expanding its footprint in Oregon. (They also had a silent partner in Kutella's father, Ron.) Orazetti had restaurant experience, which included time at McMenamins; Kutella had a degree in food and fermentation science from Oregon State University.

They were joined in 2002 by Chris Justema, who owned and managed the Tumalo Tavern in the small town of Tumalo (about six miles north of Bend). Justema had the brewery experience they needed: he had started in the industry with Rogue Ales in 1992 (when it was still based out of Ashland, Oregon, and called the Rogue Valley Brewing Company) and continued to manage Rogue's Ashland pub after the company moved to Newport on the Oregon coast. In 1997, he left Rogue to work for the Gallo Winery for three years and then moved to Bend in 2000 to open the Tumalo Tavern. By 2002,

Cascade Lakes was brewing only 1,200 barrels per year, down nearly 30 percent from its projections, and Justema was a perfect fit with his knowledge and experience in sales and the brewing industry. The brewery managed to double production and sales that year and, since then, has averaged 15 percent growth per year.

Expansion was on their minds: Orazetti and the Kutellas had purchased Bend's Cascade West Grub and Ale House, along with 50 percent of the Tumalo Tavern, acquired when Justema came on board, and they also wanted to build a restaurant and pub on Bend's west side. The original Seventh Street Brewhouse had also outgrown its original 1,300 square feet and was badly in need of expansion. In 2004, they completed both: the new Cascade Lakes Lodge opened in Bend in May 2004, and in June, they completed the teardown and rebuilding of the Seventh Street Brewhouse, which doubled its capacity. The Lodge was 6,000 square feet and offered up a full range of the brewery's beer on tap (though there was no brewery installed), as well as the restaurant space; located on Century Drive on the way to Mount Bachelor, it quickly proved a popular stop to and from the mountain.

Meanwhile, there was a quiet revolution taking place at Bend Brewing Company. In 2002, Wendi Day hired a new brewer, Tonya Cornett, who was to become one of Bend's most well-known brewers thanks to a well-honed instinct for an emerging trend in sour ales, a number of high-profile awards and a featured role in a documentary about women in the brewing industry. But that would be in the future.

Cornett grew up in Marion, Indiana, earning a bachelor's degree in psychology before moving in 1996 to Fort Collins, Colorado, where she experienced her first taste of craft beer and became hooked. She began homebrewing with a kit that had ostensibly been for her husband, Mark, and started working at H.C. Berger Brewing in Fort Collins putting together boxes and giving tours. Cornett then segued into an unpaid apprenticeship, learning the ins and outs of commercial brewing, and when Cornett and her husband moved back to Indiana in 1998, she took a brewing job at Oaken Barrel Brewing.

After three years at Oaken Barrel, Cornett decided to enroll in the Siebel Institute to further her education. Enrollment in Siebel's World Brewing Academy took her to Chicago and Germany, during which time Mark was scouting three possible "go to" states on the West Coast to move to when she returned. She graduated in 2001 and was ready for larger-scale production brewing; she wanted to apply her newly acquired knowledge to a brewing

Cascade Lakes Brewing Lodge, built in Bend in 2004. *Author's collection.*

operation beyond the scale of the brewpub. Ironic, then, that Cornett ended up accepting a job offer with Bend Brewing, but the opportunity to run the show proved too appealing. She started at the brewpub in 2002. (The recommendation for Cornett came to Wendi Day from a high school friend of Cornett's who worked for Day's cousin, who owned the Southside Pub in Bend.)

There was only a two-week overlap with the former brewer, Christian Skovborg, before Cornett took over brewhouse operations entirely. (Skovborg subsequently opened and still owns the Reed Pub in southeast Bend.) She was working fifty to sixty hours per week, brewing four batches per week and quietly improving the quality of the beer. "I do quality checks all of the time," she told the *Bend Bulletin* in a 2002 interview. "I'll even test the fermenting to detect change. From the beginning, I'll make sure it's on the right track." In addition to cleaning up the house beers (there were no master copies of any recipes, only brewing logs), she was experimenting and developing new recipes, brewing beers such as a "peach lambick [*sic*] and a razzwheat" (types of beers that would herald the styles for which she would later gain notoriety). The fruits of this labor would begin to pay off in only a few short years.

As the new millennium dawned for Deschutes Brewery, it had a strong team of brewers and had seen continual growth throughout the 1990s, even as the craft beer industry as a whole suffered a shakeout. However, the conflict between rapid growth and maintaining the integrity of a hands-on brewing process alluded to earlier in the chapter would reach its boiling point by 2003. Tony Lawrence, who would leave in November 2001 to pursue his own interests, characterized the period:

> [A]*t that particular time, it was really gelling well. The team of brewers…it was an incredible team at that point in time for Deschutes. I left to do my own thing, and everyone thought I was absolutely crazy. I mean, Gary took care of us, we were well paid, we were award-winning—it was just a beautiful, beautiful thing there. And I left to pursue my own interests…everybody thought, "What the hell are you doing Tony? We're the very best!"*

Lawrence joined Tim Gossack at Rio Salado Brewing in Arizona, where he brewed for two years before moving on to spend a year with Firestone Walker Brewing in California. He would then spend the next half decade traveling around the country as a brewing consultant and figuring out what he wanted to do next. (That would turn out to be launching Boneyard Brewing in Bend in 2010, which we will return to.)

Paul Arney was another brewer who left the company around this time, in the fall of 2002. Arney had been hired on in 1996 after putting himself through the brewing school at UC–Davis, and after six years of production brewing at Deschutes (punctuated with occasional six-week stints brewing on the downtown pub's ten-barrel system), he quit so he and his wife could follow their dream. They spent the next year and a half traveling the world. Arney returned to Deschutes in late 2004 to spend another seven years as its R&D brewmaster.

Deschutes' last round of expansion had ended in 1999, and by 2002, it was apparent that it would need to expand again. It had an output of 114,000 barrels and was distributing in ten states (Oregon, Washington, Arizona, Alaska, Montana, Idaho, California, Hawaii, Nevada and Wyoming). In order to make it to the next stage—200,000 barrels—much of 2003 was devoted to a $15 million expansion project that included the construction of a thirty-five-thousand-square-foot warehouse and a twelve-thousand-square-foot addition to the production brewery, as well as the installation of an automated German-made Huppmann brewhouse.

This automated system would be at the heart of the philosophical conflict between brewery growth and the traditional brewing process. A number of brewers simply wanted to "shovel grain and brew beer" and believed that meant having a hand in every stage of the brewing process, as opposed to pushing buttons on an automated system that removed them from much of that process. While Gary Fish could appreciate the sentiment, he also realized that in order to maintain the business as well as keep the customers happy, it simply wasn't practical to brew manually at the scale they needed. To keep up with demand, it meant automation and consistency.

Brewmaster Bill Pengelly disagreed and designed the new system to incorporate as much manual function as possible to maintain his vision of what craft beer should be. This contravened Fish's dictates for the needs of the business, and the growing pains of the past decade—the conflict between brewers wanting to maintain their hands-on relationship with the beer and the need for growth and efficiency—came to a head. Pengelly was let go in February 2003. Not surprisingly, this was quite a shakeup for the brewing staff that had been there for much of Pengelly's tenure as brewmaster, and as a result, a number of these brewers would leave over the next few years to pursue other opportunities.

Pengelly would subsequently work with Steinbart Wholesale (a division of the homebrew supply company F.H. Steinbart) and then Brewers Supply Group managing sales before retiring in 2013 and taking an instructor position with Central Oregon Community College's Continuing Education program, teaching a brewing course geared toward preparing students for the Institute of Brewing and Distilling (IBD) General Certificate in Brewing.

In Pengelly's absence, the head brewer role fell first to Mark Henion and then Paul Cook while the company looked for a new brewmaster. Henion had joined Deschutes Brewery in 1995, Cook in 2000, and both of them would ultimately depart Deschutes by 2005. The search for a new brewmaster encompassed the rest of 2003 as the brewery continued with its expansion, and by the time the year was out, both efforts were complete. Deschutes had significantly increased its capacity and had added Larry Sidor as its new brewmaster.

Sidor had a long history in the industry: he had graduated from Oregon State University in the mid-1970s with a degree in food science and fermentation, with a minor in oenology (he was one of the first fermentation science graduates from the school). He went to work for Olympia Brewing in Tumwater, Washington, in 1974. During his twenty-three-year career at Olympia, Sidor worked his way up from washing tanks and kegs to the

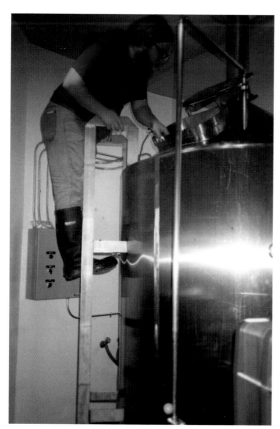

Left: John Harris checking on the progress of the boil of a batch of beer. *Courtesy Deschutes Brewery.*

Below: Deschutes Brewery's production plant. *Courtesy Deschutes Brewery.*

Above: Silver Moon Brewing founder Tyler Reichert. *Author's collection.*

Left: Cascade Lakes Brewing beers. *Photo by James Jaggard. Courtesy Wanderlust Tours.*

McMenamins Old St. Francis School, present day. *Courtesy McMenamins.*

McMenamins Old St. Francis School basement brewery. *Courtesy McMenamins.*

Above: Below Grade Brewing serving beer at the NorthWest Crossing farmers' market. *Author's collection.*

Right: GoodLife Brewing opened its doors in 2011. *Author's collection.*

Left: Paul Arney of the Ale Apothecary. *Author's collection.*

Below: The ten-hectoliter Japanese brewhouse at Crux Fermentation Project. *Author's collection.*

Wild Ride Brewing, Redmond, Oregon's newest brewery. *Author's collection.*

The annual Bend Brew Fest takes place every August in the Les Schwab Amphitheater. *Author's collection.*

Above: The Little Woody Barrel-Aged Brew Fest packs the parking lot of the Des Chutes Historical Museum every Labor Day weekend. *Author's collection.*

Left: The Little Woody festival allows patrons to sample specialty wood-aged beers. *Author's collection.*

Silipints, silicone pint glasses. These particular ones have been awarded as prizes for those who complete the Bend Ale Trail. *Author's collection.*

The Cycle Pub provides a unique beer-and-pedaling experience as it tours Bend breweries. *Author's collection.*

The Growler Guys was the first dedicated growler fill station in Oregon. *Author's collection.*

Every year, Deschutes Brewery picks fresh hops in the Willamette Valley for its Hop Trip fresh-hop ale. *Courtesy Deschutes Brewery.*

Deschutes Brewery Public House at night. *Courtesy Deschutes Brewery.*

10 Barrel Brewing serves up a wide variety of beer at its pub, including this Coconut Curry Pumpkin Ale. *Author's collection.*

Brewers Jimmy Seifrit of 10 Barrel and Curt Plants of GoodLife. *Author's collection.*

McMenamins Old St. Francis School brewer Mike White, with avid fan Paul Carrington. *Author's collection.*

Open fermenters at Crux Fermentation Project. *Author's collection.*

Worthy Brewing grows hops on its property, as well as herbs in its Hop House. *Author's collection.*

The Growler Guys fill a large number of growlers on any given day. *Author's collection.*

Tasting beer at the Ale Apothecary's mountain brewery. *Author's collection.*

Sampling barrel-aged Mirror Mirror Barleywine from Deschutes Brewery. *Author's collection.*

Bottles of Tough Love, a barrel-aged imperial stout from Crux Fermentation Project. *Author's collection.*

Right: McMenamins' Thundercone Fresh Hop Ale, brewed each year in a special "running of the brewers" to collect the hops. *Author's collection.*

Below: Fresh-hop beers abound at the annual Sisters Fresh Hop Festival. *Author's collection.*

Samples of beer from Worthy Brewing. *Author's collection.*

A collection of Jubelale beers featuring labels from each year up through 2011, on display at Deschutes Brewery. *Courtesy Deschutes Brewery.*

brewmaster position ("You name it, I did it," said Sidor in an interview), witnessing the buyout of Olympia by G. Heileman Brewing Company in 1983 and then Stroh Brewing in 1996. In 1997, Sidor left Olympia and took a job with S.S. Steiner, a hop dealer based out of Yakima, Washington, and purchased a small vineyard on the side to make wine. His seven years with S.S. Steiner exposed him to all facets of the hop industry, and while there, Sidor helped to revolutionize the production of hop pellets (perhaps ironically, as Sidor prefers to brew with whole-leaf hops). Deschutes Brewery contacted Sidor in 2003 about its open brewmaster position, and to Sidor it seemed like a perfect fit. He started with the brewery in January 2004.

Sidor's approach to brewing embraced a "push the envelope" attitude to brewing creativity while maintaining strict controls to protect the integrity of the beer with respect to the customer—precisely what Deschutes needed at the time. Paul Arney, who returned to Deschutes later that year, wrote that Sidor "was pushing the brewing into new commercial realms and encouraging our brewers to find any and all boundaries (so we could subsequently break them)."

Meanwhile, McMenamins was renovating the downtown St. Francis School property, planning for a fall of 2004 opening. The timing was right, as much of downtown Bend had been going through its own revitalization over the previous few years (projects that included the new library, the Tower Theatre, the St. Clair Place building and development of upscale, boutique dining like the Blacksmith and Merenda Restaurants). McMenamins preserved much of the historic character of the old school, with old photographs and local artwork emphasizing the property's history, and converted old classrooms into the main hotel lodging. The front of that main building housed the main pub and restaurant. A second building housed the theater, a soaking pool, event and dining space and an additional pub lounge. At the back of the property, four older bungalow houses were converted into additional lodging, and a garage was turned into a small pub and cigar bar, O'Kane's, named after early Bend personality Hugh O'Kane (who owned a number of early saloons and a hotel).

The old school itself had dated to the Great Depression, the first parochial school built in Central Oregon, and it was the realization of the dream of Catholic priest Father Luke Sheehan, who had come to Central Oregon in 1910 from County Cork, Ireland. Sheehan and his nephew, Father Dominic O'Connor, who arrived in 1922, were part of the Irish Capuchin order of Catholic priests and established the St. Francis parish under the Baker Diocese. Sheehan's work was challenging, as Catholics were a minority

The original St. Francis School, circa 1950. *Courtesy McMenamins.*

Rear of Silver Moon Brewing, downtown Bend. *Author's collection.*

in Central Oregon, and prejudice against them was common—so much so that there was a resurgence in the Ku Klux Klan during the 1920s. Its goals in Oregon primarily involved the suppression of Catholic influence. The Klan in Bend burned crosses on Pilot Butte, vandalized the Catholic church and St. Charles Hospital and marched in robes around the church. Sheehan, accompanied by a number of Irish sheepherders and parishioners, confronted the Klan at one of its meetings and defused the situation, and the local Klan presence disbanded shortly thereafter. This had been the last major obstacle (other than money, of course) in the establishment of a parochial school, and in 1936, the four-classroom St. Francis School opened to 145 students.

McMenamins worked closely with the community in the redevelopment of the school to preserve much of the character of the property, even bringing in former teachers and students for their historical perspective and to share the progress of the renovation. In November 2004, the Old St. Francis School opened its doors, and Central Oregon welcomed its fifth brewery to the region.

The brewery was located in the basement of the main building, below the restaurant, and consisted of a six-barrel system using glycol-jacketed Grundy tanks for fermenters. Brewing duties on the small basement system were conducted by Dave Fleming, who had gotten his start in the industry in 1992 with BridgePort Brewing before moving to the Lucky Lab brewpub in Portland in 1994. Fleming left the Lucky Lab in 2002 and worked stints with Rock Bottom Brewing in Bellevue, Washington; Caldera Brewing in Ashland, Oregon; and even a short time at Bend Brewing before launching the brewery at the Old St. Francis School.

At the same time the Old St. Francis School was opening, Tyler Reichert over at Silver Moon Brewing was in the process of relocating his brewery and the Brew Shop (renamed that year from the Home Brewer) from its Division Street location on Bend's north side to a new location on Greenwood Avenue on the edge of downtown. The brewing system was upgraded as well. Reichert had purchased a like-new seven-barrel system from a San Francisco restaurant that had ultimately been uninterested in brewing. The new location had 6,400 square feet, with half of that devoted to brewing (compared to a brewing footprint of 700 square feet at the old location), and once the new brewery was up and running, Reichert turned over the brewing duties to Tyler West.

The retail half of the business was located in the front of the building, sharing the space with a small tasting room bar. The homebrewing community in the region was thriving, and the homebrew supply portion of the business accounted for about 50 percent of Reichert's business, although that number would shrink as Silver Moon Brewing grew.

With five breweries and brewpubs in Central Oregon and the region's largest city, Bend, having a population of only about sixty thousand, some wondered if such a number was supportable. Many believed not only that it was sustainable but also that there was room for more; at the end of 2004, the *Bulletin* ran an article exploring this issue:

> *The number of microbrew pubs in Bend could still increase, experts said. "At heart, they are nothing more than a restaurant that makes great beer," said [Association of Brewers director Paul] Gatza. "If there's room for another bar, there is room for another brew pub. They are simply adding in the component of freshly made beer."*
>
> *"People enjoy beer as part of a healthy social life and enjoy being served by someone happy, upbeat and knowledgeable about the intrinsic qualities of beer," [Odell Brewing vice-president John] Bryant said. "Beer is about culture and people, and if you do both well, that's what it's about."*
>
> *Gary Fish, president of Deschutes Brewery, agreed. "I welcome anyone to town as long as they're good," he said. "Bend could handle a few more brew pubs. Beer is culture. We could use a lot more of it in our society."*

Prescient words. Within a decade's time, Central Oregon would not just have a "few more brew pubs." Rather, beer would become a significant line item in the regional economy. In the meantime, the region's five pioneers—Deschutes Brewery, Cascade Lakes Brewing, Bend Brewing, Silver Moon Brewing and McMenamins Old St. Francis School—continued to follow an upward curve of growth and quality that helped to pave the way for the coming explosion.

CHAPTER 6
THE SECOND WAVE

In 2003, twin brothers Chris and Jeremy Cox were tired of the corporate business world and were seeking a change. The brothers, originally from Lincoln City, Oregon, had graduated from Oregon State University and were working "for the man up in Portland in the corporate world." They were ready for something new. Casting about for ideas and opportunities, they settled on two possibilities:

> *It came down to a drift boat company or a bar, and the drift boat company was too expensive; we didn't have any money. So the bar was super reasonable. We never worked in bars before or anything. We just wanted to get to Bend; we couldn't find any other way to get to Bend to get jobs, so we bought a bar.*

They purchased Lucy's Place, a small bar and diner located downtown, and renamed it JC's Bar and Grill. For the first year of ownership, they still worked their corporate jobs in Portland during the week (in software sales and business consulting), drove to Bend on Fridays to work the bar for the three-day weekend and then went back to Portland to start the process over again.

Although the brothers had no bar experience or background in the beer industry, they had the business acumen, a desire to learn and a willingness to take risks, and JC's was a successful venture, proving to be a popular nightlife destination. And while they learned some hard lessons that first year, their overall timing was excellent, as Bend was in the middle of an economic boom fueled by the growth resulting from the influx of newcomers who had discovered Bend over the past decade. While tourism still accounted for the lion's share of the regional economy, construction and real estate had become significant contributors as well, fueled by a growing population that needed housing combined with the low interest rates and easy lending fostered by the national housing boom.

The Cox brothers loved craft beer, but the idea to start a brewery wasn't born with the purchase of the bar. The seeds were planted in 2004, during the time that McMenamins was renovating the St. Francis School in downtown Bend, a stone's throw away from JC's. Chris Cox related the story in an interview:

> *Actually, the McMenamin brothers* [Mike and Brian] *were the ones that kind of got us into it. They were opening up McMenamins at the time; they'd come over and sit at our bar, and Jeremy and I worked every single day—one of us would cook and one of us would bartend. So we got to know them pretty well because they would come in every day, have a beer, have lunch, 'cause it was right across the street. And we just admired what they did. They knew that we really liked craft beer at the time, so we started talking to them about it, getting more excited about the opportunity about opening a brewery, and that was how it worked out.*

The idea continued to percolate through 2005 and into 2006, even as some in Bend questioned whether five breweries represented a saturation of the market. Despite those doubts, the local beer industry was forging ahead and looking stronger than ever during that time.

Deschutes Brewery, under the direction of new brewmaster Larry Sidor, continued to grow and increased the output of its specialty beers, to much critical acclaim. A year-round lineup of limited-run pub-specialty beers in twenty-two-ounce bottles, its Bond Street Series appeared in the spring of 2005, followed up by a fall release of the groundbreaking Hop Trip fresh hop ale (brewed with hops harvested that same day). The year 2006 saw the addition of Inversion IPA to its year-round lineup (it dominated the market), as well as the first release each of Hop Henge (its experimental imperial IPA) and the new Reserve Series line, The Abyss (a beer that would subsequently draw much acclaim and awards). That year, it also introduced a company-wide sensory program to help ensure the quality of the beer.

Deschutes brewer Mark Henion left the company in March 2005 and joined Cascade Lakes Brewing in Redmond. Desiring to "shovel grain and brew beer" (as characterized by owner Chris Justema), Henion took a position in the cellaring department and worked his way up to become head brewer. Joining Henion from Deschutes was John Van Duzer, another longtime veteran who had started in the mid-1990s at around the same time as Henion. Cascade Lakes was expanding in the meantime as well, adding two fifty-barrel fermenters and two bright tanks in 2005 to increase its capacity to 3,400 barrels annually (up from 1,200 a few years before), and a new bottling line arrived in 2006 (purchased from California's Lost Coast Brewery).

Tonya Cornett at Bend Brewing Company was consistently improving the core lineup of beers at the brewpub, as well as introducing seasonals such as Apricot Summer Ale, Axe Head Red and HopHead Imperial IPA. The HopHead in particular was a popular beer, so much so that the brewpub began offering it in twenty-two-ounce bottles, available at the pub only in 2005. In 2006, the beer won the gold medal in the coveted "American-Style India Pale Ale" category at the Great American Beer Festival—the first such medal for Bend Brewing, as well as a sudden thrust into the brewing spotlight for Cornett. She would follow up with a win in 2007 with a silver GABF medal for Outback X (a double, or strong, version of the brewpub's popular Outback Old Ale), and Bend Brewing would go on to win at least one medal per year subsequently.

The GABF medals were followed by an even more prestigious award for Cornett in 2008. At the Brewers Association's World Beer Cup, Bend Brewing and Cornett won the Champion Brewery and Brewmaster award in the "Small Brewpub" category. Even more significantly, Cornett was the first female brewmaster ever to do so.

Meanwhile, Silver Moon Brewing had settled into its new location, downtown Bend on Greenwood Avenue, and owner Tyler Reichert brought in Evan Taylor as assistant brewer to Tyler West in mid-2005. Taylor was a homebrewer who had started out volunteering at Silver Moon, splitting his time between the brewery and the homebrew shop before being hired on full time. The Brew Shop continued to be located in the front of the building, sharing space with the tasting room for the brewery; later that year, Reichert added tables and chairs, as well as a pool table, and began selling beer on-premise, offering samples and selling it to go. Unfortunately, the business's retail sales permit did not allow for on-site sales, and in December, they were temporarily suspended until they could bring the space up to spec to allow alcohol sales. For most of 2006, Silver Moon was unable to sell beer until the retail license issues, like the construction of a second bathroom, were resolved, but by that December, it was able to again serve beer.

The kettle and mash tun at Bend Brewing Company. Current head brewer Ian Larkin brews award-winning beers in tight quarters. *Author's collection.*

Over at McMenamins Old St. Francis School, the brewing duties had been handed over to Mike White at the beginning of 2006. White had been with McMenamins since December 1997, working his way up from being a pubster and bartender to managing several pubs before moving into brewing in April 2004 at McMenamins' Fulton Pub in Portland. White's first real exposure to craft beer had been in the mid-1990s, attending college in Salem and visiting the McMenamins Thompson Pub. "Seriously, the first time we went there, I was almost certain they were playing a joke on me," said White. "They sent me in with this Mason jar; I was almost positive that they were pulling a prank on me. 'How am I gonna get beer in this?'" During his first full year at the Old St. Francis School brewery, White ran all of the brewery operations himself without any help and brewed 1,091 barrels on the 6-barrel system. In the following years, he would bring on a seasonal brewer during the summer months to help share the burden. (And as of this writing, the Old St. Francis School is the only McMenamins brewery that staffs only one brewer for nine months of the year.)

But as much as anything, it would be the Cox brothers who would be the vanguard for the next big shift in the Bend craft brewing scene. Their idea of starting their own brewery had continued to simmer, and when brewer Paul Cook left Deschutes Brewery in 2005, he joined with the brothers to bring that dream to reality and formed a new brewing company, Wildfire Brewing, which they announced in November 2006. They installed a ten-barrel, former sake brewing system that Cook had acquired from Japan in a small 1,600-square-foot industrial space on the northeast side of Bend, and by late March 2007, they had started brewing the first batches of beer, destined to go on tap at JC's. The first two beers in the lineup were Code 24 Pale Ale and Logger Lager, which were on tap by late April, and those were soon followed by Backdraft IPA. Central Oregon now had six brewing operations.

JC's was their primary outlet and carried the full lineup of Wildfire beers, and they gradually worked on getting the beer on tap elsewhere in town. Although they had initially hoped to tap into the lager market, they realized that the Logger Lager was ultimately a failure in sales and instead focused on selling the pale ale and later the IPA, both of which were more suited to the local palates seeking out hoppier beers. Even so, they encountered some resistance early on from restaurants and bar owners who thought that a fourth local brewery competing for tap handles might represent an oversaturation of the market (their main local competition was with Deschutes, Cascade Lakes and Silver Moon, as Bend Brewing and McMenamins were brewpubs that did not distribute outside their own establishments).

In fact, the opposite appeared to be true, with those in the community who were beginning to think that the local beer market had room for a lot more. In part, this was because craft beer growth had recovered since the shakeout of the late '90s, and in part, it was because it was a lifestyle statement. In general, choosing craft beer over the national brands had been a lifestyle choice since the rise of the craft beer movement in the '70s and '80s, and although a previous chapter suggested a link between the Central Oregon lifestyle and enjoying premium, quality beer, by 2007, it was being explicitly recognized that there was a (perhaps inextricable?) relationship between the two. The idea, in other words, was that in choosing to live in Central Oregon, one was also choosing the beer. The *Bulletin* explored this idea in April 2007, just before Wildfire opened:

> *To recognize the good life in Bend, one need only spot a few accessories: a suntan, a dog, a baby in a fancy jogging stroller and, depending on the time of day, a mug of specialty coffee or a pint of fresh, locally made beer. Yes, beer.*

Central Oregon is barreling toward a future where brew pubs are as plentiful as specialty coffee shops and golf courses.

Between [the six brewing companies], *Bend has one brew pub for every 12,548 residents.*

But don't expect Bend to set any national records just yet.

"There are certainly places that are much more saturated than Bend," [Brewers Association spokesperson Julia] *Herz said.*

That could mean that Bend is still a long way from quenching its thirst for locally made brew.

The economics backed it up. Even as the economy was slowing down by that time—the "Great Recession" would officially hit in December 2007 and last through June 2009, although Bend would be hit harder than the rest of the country due to the collapse of the housing bubble—craft beer accounted for about 13 percent of all beer sales in the region, more than double most of the rest of the country at 6 percent. This was further evident not only with the opening of Wildfire but also with the other breweries. Deschutes announced plans early in 2007 to open a second brewpub in Portland, which would open the following year to great acclaim, in time for the brewery's twentieth anniversary. Silver Moon sold the homebrew retail portion of the business, the Brew Shop, to Tom Gilles in mid-2007 in order to turn its tasting room space into a brewpub and focus on expanding its production. Gilles, a longtime homebrewer and former postal worker, moved the shop back to its former location on Division Street and expanded its offerings, including adding a sizable bottle shop portion selling specialty beers. Gilles and his partners, Jeff Hawes, Glen Samuel and Randy Woodbridge, would be able to bring a renewed enthusiasm to the homebrew shop and support to the community, something that had perhaps been lacking in recent months at Silver Moon as the brewery portion of the business had grown.

Cascade Lakes Brewing in Redmond closed the original tasting room located in its production brewery in 2007 in order to maximize its own production. Although sales for the Redmond brewery were flat in 2007 (the first time since the new owners had taken over several years before), it came back strong in 2008 and won its first medal at the Great American Beer Festival for its Blonde Bombshell, a golden ale that was hugely popular among the recreation-minded in Central Oregon.

In June 2007, barely two months after Wildfire Brewing started brewing its first beers, Wade Underwood, a recent newcomer to the town of Sisters, announced plans to open a brewpub there as part of the town's new

FivePine development (which would feature a lodge, cottages, a spa and a conference center, as well as a movie theater and the Sisters Athletic Club). It would be the first brewing company for the small town that sat near the western edge of Deschutes County under the sweeping vistas of the Cascade Mountains. (Though it was perhaps not strictly the first; in the 1990s, there was a restaurant named the Sisters Brewing Company that was rumored to have had a selection of brewed-on-premise beers for a very short period of time. A visit by the author in the late '90s revealed the opposite to be true, however, and there is no corroborating source to substantiate this claim.) Although Sisters had a population of only 959 as of the year 2000 (this would increase to 1,706 by 2008), it sat on the east–west route in and out of Central Oregon over the mountains via the Santiam Pass, and as such, it was host to much of the traffic traveling through the entire region. That fact and its situation as a gateway to the abundant recreational possibilities offered by the national forest and high lakes country resulted in a vibrant tourism industry. Locating a brewpub in the town, though there might be some question as to how well it would fare in the off season, was almost a given considering the area's growing fixation on craft beer.

Even so, Underwood had his doubts. "I thought we were late to the game," he said in an interview. "That was one of my concerns before we opened: 'Man there's already a lot of them; I'm glad I'm not going into Bend. I don't want to go into Redmond. We'll be the only ones here. We're late to the game,' and boy was I proven wrong." Underwood had grown up in Beaverton, Oregon, before attending college at the University of Oregon. After college, he moved around "chasing careers" and ended up working in Phoenix, Arizona, for eight years, working in business and operations and thinking about craft beer, which he had first discovered at a McMenamins pub in Beaverton:

> *McMenamins was really growing up at the time, and there was a strip-mall pub half a mile from my house* [in Beaverton]. *That's where I kind of got into the, "Oh wow, you can do all kinds of crazy things with beer!" And it's not this shotgunning-with-my-buddies stuff, it's really interesting flavor profiles, and how do you get this black thing into a beer that tastes good too. And to be honest, I really, really missed it when I was in Phoenix.*

Underwood had wanted to be his own boss, so even though he had no background in brewing or restaurants, he had written up a business plan for a brewpub. Initially, he planned for the brewpub to open in Phoenix, but he realized that he did not want to live there anymore. So, he and his wife moved to Central Oregon in mid-2006 and chose Sisters for its small-town, community feel—that and the fact that the town had no breweries.

Ground was broken on January 7, 2008, with an official name: Three Creeks Brewing Company. It would consist of a ten-barrel brewery, brewpub and restaurant, with a rustic, Old West livery stable theme (much like the touristy Old West theme of the rest of the town of Sisters) and a planned summer opening. Underwood had contacted and hired brewer Dave Fleming, who had helped to launch the brewery at the McMenamins Old St. Francis School in Bend and who had been working at the Lucky Lab Brewpub in Portland since leaving McMenamins in 2006. The brewpub officially opened on July 21, 2008, with three beers initially: Knotty Blonde, Old Prospector Pale Ale and 8 Second India Black Ale. (Those first three beers were brewed by Wildfire Brewing under contract with Three Creeks, as its new brewery equipment hadn't yet been installed.) Additional beers to join the lineup in the coming weeks included Firestorm Red, Anvil Amber and Stonefly Rye.

The timing was fortuitous: the flush economic boom years of the first half of the decade had been unsustainable, and the slowdown of the economy and onset of the Great Recession at the end of 2007 heralded a crash that would settle into Central Oregon—and Bend in particular—by the middle of 2008. Three Creeks had opened just in time; Underwood asked his banker six months later what the result would have been had he tried to get funding for the brewpub at that time (the end of 2008). The answer: "You would never get through the door with that business plan! We wouldn't finance it; there's no way we would finance it!"

Bend's recent growth had fueled the construction and real estate that led to a local housing bubble that was much more pronounced than what was occurring elsewhere. This housing bubble was fueled by speculation, low interest rates and easy home loans and led to a glut of construction and significantly overvalued properties. Then came the crash. "Home values got cut in half," wrote Ben Jacklet in *Oregon Business* magazine in 2011. "Unemployment soared to over 16%. A once-promising aviation sector imploded. So did an overheated market for destination resorts. Brokers, builders and speculators once flush with cash woke up underwater and flailing. Banks renowned for their no-document, easy-money loans stopped lending. Layoffs led to notices of default; foreclosure brought bankruptcy."

The crash affected almost everything in Bend—although surprisingly (or perhaps *un*surprisingly), the craft beer industry was among the least affected and continued to grow, albeit more slowly. This prompted many to wonder if beer was recession-proof; an online *Inc. Magazine* article from 2009 opined that "recession-weary consumers seek out small luxuries during tough times" when examining the rising sales of craft brewers (as opposed to the downturn experienced by the major corporate brewers). Regardless of the reasons, Three Creeks met with success in Sisters (although it noted a downturn in the restaurant side of the business). Wildfire had grown through its first year and had brought on Brad Wales (formerly of High Desert Beverage Distributors and who had started Bachelor Beverage Company in the 1980s) and his son Garrett Wales as co-owners, and Deschutes Brewery increased its output from 162,000 barrels in 2007 to 180,000 barrels in 2008. Other breweries saw similar growth at their own levels.

The addition of the Waleses as co-owners of Wildfire Brewing added valuable experience in distribution and pub management, although the young brewing company faced another hurdle in the latter half of 2008 in the form of a trademark violation notice: the Wildfire Restaurant chain, which had locations back east in Illinois, Minnesota and Virginia, advised the brewery of its trademarked name and suggested that it change the name within six months or face a court battle. Wildfire Brewing opted to change its name, and in December, it announced the new moniker: 10 Barrel Brewing Company. It became official in January 2009.

Also in December 2008, as an apt illustration of craft beer in the face of a down economy, Tony Lawrence announced his intentions to open an eighth brewing company in Central Oregon. As reported by the *Bulletin*:

> *The Brewtal Brewing Co., formed by Bend resident Tony Lawrence, will be the region's eighth brewing company. Lawrence began moving into a small warehouse near downtown Bend on Tuesday and will begin building the brewery he hopes will fill its first keg this spring.*
>
> *"I'll be brewing ales, like most craft breweries do, IPAs, pale ales,"* *Lawrence said. "Some guys are over the top heavy-handed with hops, but that's not my school. I'm a more traditional, balanced brewer."*

Lawrence had left Deschutes Brewery late in 2001 to pursue other opportunities and had joined another former Deschutes brewer, Tim Gossack, at Gossack's Rio Salado Brewing in Tempe, Arizona. He left Rio Salado in 2004 and returned to his home state of California, looking for the next opportunity, and he had lined up an interview with Lagunitas Brewing (and several other places). A fortuitous stop for a beer with Matt Brynildson at

Firestone Walker Brewing in Paso Robles, California, led to a yearlong stint with that brewery, working with the packaging department to help develop a different level of quality control (as well as on other projects, though not brewing beer). He realized after six months that he did not enjoy his role there, although he acknowledged in retrospect that this time provided some of the most invaluable industry experience of his career.

After exactly one year with Firestone Walker, Lawrence returned to Bend to, among other things, fix up his rental home. But he was also looking for opportunities beyond the salaried job track—some way to reinvent how he could stay afloat in the industry. A chance meeting with his friend Nick Floyd of Indiana's Three Floyds Brewing at the 2006 Craft Brewers Conference in Seattle provided an answer, as Floyd was in need of brewing help and asked if Lawrence could be on a plane to Indiana the following week. He could and did, and he helped Three Floyds in a number of different areas over the next few years, flying out several times a year to spend up to three or four months with the brewery. This consulting role led to his formation of Brewtal Industries, through which he consulted on brewing, installation and fabrication for Three Floyds and a number of other breweries around the country and the world.

Over those years, he had gradually been collecting used brewing components, much of it scavenged from breweries' "boneyards" of discarded equipment, often with a thought toward piecing together his own brewery in Bend. His goals were modest:

> I'm just a lifelong brewer that acquired some five-barrel system and hoarded it out in my garage until I had some more bits and pieces of equipment and thought, maybe I can find a way to make a five-barrel batch of beer. It was never financially or volume based; maybe if I can just make some beer, pay the lease on the building and hopefully be able to pay my mortgage; that's success—doing what you love.

Despite the growth of craft beer in the down economy, the way forward would be anything but easy. Lawrence had been looking for space to install his five-barrel brewhouse and several fermenters and happened upon Clay and Melodee Storey. The Storeys had themselves been casualties of the housing crash that hit hard in 2008. Originally from Corbett, Oregon, they had moved to Bend in 1991 following high school to take advantage of the skiing and snowboarding opportunities offered by Mount Bachelor. Clay Storey had subcontracted with a company called Hearth Appliances, selling

Boneyard Brewing, one of Oregon's fastest-growing breweries, in its original location. *Author's collection.*

hearths and stoves of all types, and in 1999, Storey started his own business, Gutter Guys, selling rain gutters. They had prospered during the first half of the decade, along with the rest of the construction industry, but when the market collapsed, they ultimately had to lay off their employees and reduce their footprint. Sensing that brewing beer was a better investment than renting to others in the building industry, they leased space out in their building to Lawrence.

Lawrence began the installation of his brewing operation, but because he was frequently traveling for consulting jobs, progress was slow. By June 2009, Storey had approached Lawrence with an offer: Lawrence needed a partner since he was on the road all the time; Storey had the business experience to complement Lawrence's brewing experience; and lacking work, Storey could dedicate all of his time to getting the brewery up and running. Lawrence asked Storey what he knew about selling beer. "I sell rain gutters in the desert; I'm not gonna have a problem selling beer!" said Storey. Lawrence was convinced.

The next year was slow going and tough; no money was coming in, Lawrence was guiding Storey on how to build a brewery over the phone from the road and they had virtually no support, financial or otherwise. Storey sold his Gutter Guys business to a competitor, and that sale provided just enough cash flow to finish the brewery. By the time it was complete, in April 2010, they had just enough money to purchase a load of malt, enough for two beers: Black 13 and Bone-a-Fide Pale Ale. They planned their debut by sponsoring the National Beard and Moustache Championships, which came to Bend on June 5 of that year; this necessitated borrowing additional money, but they sold out of their first two beers and a third, Girl Beer, that weekend. Boneyard Brewing was officially the region's eighth brewery (and the sixth for Bend alone).

Meanwhile, 10 Barrel's head brewer, Paul Cook, had departed in 2009 for Ninkasi Brewing in Eugene, Oregon, and brewing duties had been taken over by Dan Olsen. Olsen was a veteran of Deschutes Brewery (he started there in 2000), and by May of that year, he had been joined by Thom Tash, who came from Kona Brewing in Hawaii. Under their tenure, the brewery won its first Great American Beer Festival medal, a bronze, for its S1NIST0R Black Ale.

Although 10 Barrel had a loyal following and a successful presence in Central Oregon, the owners themselves were not making any money—it all went back into the business. That began to change when 10 Barrel's beer was picked up by a distributor that brought its beers to Portland in mid-2009. The beer was a hit in Portland, and as sales increased, the owners realized that this new market could take the business to the next level—even become profitable. They decided to take a new leap, a risky one in the current economic climate, and in August 2009, they announced plans for their own brewpub, to be opened on Bend's west side. It was to be located in a former bakery, a three-thousand-square-foot space that would not house an actual brewing system but would be an outlet for the brewery's full lineup, as well as special draft-only offerings. The pub opened in February 2010, and any doubts about opening a restaurant and pub in the down economy were put to rest, as it was an immediate success.

There were personnel changes taking place in the brewing staffs of Cascade Lakes and Silver Moon during that time as well. Mark Henion departed Cascade Lakes, bound for Ninkasi Brewing, and when he left, he wrote a long letter to the Redmond brewery detailing what it needed to do in order to change and improve. Cascade Lakes was still using the original brewhouse cobbled together from used dairy tanks in 1994, so it set out to implement Henion's advice. It would take nearly two years to do

10 Barrel Brewing Pub. *Author's collection.*

so, culminating in 2011 with a big remodel and expansion built around a twenty-five-barrel, custom JV Northwest brewing system. (Tony Lawrence had helped them reconfigure the entire catwalk around the new brewery in exchange for an old bright tank.) John Van Duzer, a Deschutes alumnus who had come to Cascade Lakes with Henion in 2005, stepped into the head brewer role in Henion's absence.

At Silver Moon Brewing, Evan Taylor, assistant brewer to Tyler West who had been with the brewery for three and half years, left in the spring of 2009 to take a similar position at Montana Brewing in Billings. During his time at Silver Moon, he had completed his associates degree in brewing science at the Siebel Institute, and Taylor became head brewer at Montana Brewing in 2010. To replace Taylor, owner Tyler Reichert hired Lorren "LoLo" Lancaster, who had spent time with Anderson Valley Brewing in California and Deschutes Brewery and was one of the original owners of the Green Dragon pub in Portland before it was bought by Rogue Ales. Although Lancaster would be with the brewery for only a few months before departing, he would pop up again the following year in connection with a new brewpub opening.

In the meantime, head brewer Tyler West had his hands full and needed a new assistant brewer, and he suggested Brett Thomas, a homebrewer who had been laid off from his job at Bend Memorial Clinic earlier that summer in 2009. Thomas had moved to Bend in 2005 from Las Vegas and had been instrumental in establishing a new homebrew club, the Central Oregon Homebrewers Organization (COHO). Thomas was a homebrewer's homebrewer: he had been brewing since 1997, with a particular focus on the creativity and science behind the beer and a close attention to details, particularly regarding the raw materials and the nuances between them. Perfection and consistency were what he sought. "I'm gonna make sixteen batches of American Cream Ale until I find what I'm looking for!" he laughingly said in an interview. When he was laid off, he spent the summer consuming technical brewing books and brewing batch after batch to hone his skills, all with a notion of being in the craft beer industry in some capacity. One day while at Silver Moon talking with Tyler West, West suggested he brew a batch of beer with himself and Lancaster. Thomas readily accepted, and although most of his duties for that first batch consisted of the grunt work—dragging hoses around the brewery, cleaning the mash tun—his first commercial batch of beer was in the books: Silver Moon's Twisted Gourd Pumpkin Ale. When West suggested Thomas for the assistant brewer role in the wake of Lancaster's departure, owner Tyler Reichert hired him on. West and Thomas proved to be a great team, and over the next several years, starting in 2010, Silver Moon would win its first GABF medals (some of which were for beers based on Thomas's recipes).

Over at McMenamins Old St. Francis School, there was a sea change underway. For a number of years, McMenamins' beer reputation "had kind of gone by the wayside," acknowledged Brian McMenamin, due to a lack of focus, tight cost controls and drinkers who perhaps had viewed the brewpub chain as stagnant and had moved on to newer and different beers and breweries. By the latter half of the decade, the company had recognized these issues and made a conscious effort to turn things around. It removed cost controls that had been restraining the brewers and gave them freer rein in their brewing. Old St. Francis brewer Mike White summed up the feeling from the brewers' perspective:

> They've always been good about giving us freedom to make whatever we want…as long as we stayed under these constraints. And now it's like… they took some of those handcuffs off, and now we're like, "All right! Let's get barrels in here, let's buy this, let's buy that! I'm gonna use that European

hop, you know, or I'm gonna use this European malt. I'm gonna make an imperial stout with it!"

White had been quietly brewing quality, consistent beers since taking over the brewery in 2006, and with the cost controls removed, he had more freedom to innovate and improve the beers even further. (A similar story was unfolding at other McMenamins breweries.)

By mid-2010, there were eight regional brewing operations producing beer, three of which had only opened over the past three years, and despite that number, there would be three more breweries announced before the year was out. The first of these to be announced was Noble Brewing in June.

The seeds for Noble Brewing were sown back in the early 2000s, when friends and roommates Ty Barnett and Curt Plants were introduced to homebrewing by a friend. Not satisfied with their first batch (a stovetop kit they purchased from the Brew Shop), they decided for their second batch to dive in headfirst, building a three-tier, ten-gallon all-grain brewing system. Homebrewing led to talk about opening an Irish-themed pub someday, which in turn led to a business plan. Running the numbers, they began to wonder: what if they attached a brewery to their pub?

When the economy began to collapse and futures were uncertain (Barnett was in restaurant management, and Plants was a personal trainer), they realized that if they wanted to open a brewery, they should do it professionally. That meant training and experience, so Plants enrolled in the Siebel Institute, while Barnett took a general manager job at a restaurant in Cannon Beach, Oregon. After completing Siebel, Plants went to work at Rogue Ales in Newport, Oregon, and within three months he was assistant head brewer, working side by side with Rogue's brewmaster, John Maier. During that time, Plants was developing recipes and brewing test batches on their ten-gallon homebrew system, and Maier would offer feedback.

On their days off, Barnett and Plants would meet halfway, at the Pelican Pub in Pacific City, to discuss their business plans. After nearly two years, they determined that the time was right. They had decided that they wanted to open a fifteen-barrel production brewery in Bend, but by that time, Wildfire and Three Creeks had opened. Thinking that the market might be tapped for beer, they considered other locations: Kalispell, Montana; Vancouver, Washington; Washington's Tri-Cities area; Medford, Oregon; and Whitefish, Montana. Each location had its appeal, but their friends and family were in Bend, and they realized, "Everything's right about Bend." So, they returned in 2009 to begin the process of lining up investors and seeking a location to house their brewery.

Through a friend of a friend, Barnett and Plants met Pratt Rather, an industry veteran who helped to start SweetWater Brewing in Atlanta, Georgia, as well as Everybody's Brewing in White Salmon, Washington. Rather had the business and investment acumen that proved invaluable, and he became a third partner in the venture. By 2010, the planned brewery capacity had grown from fifteen to thirty barrels, and they were ready to sign a lease on a building in northeast Bend (a space formerly occupied by BMC Choppers) when that deal fell through at the last minute. Negotiations began on a large space in the Century Center, a mixed-use development on the west side of Bend, which was a former indoor tennis court; by February 2011, they had begun renovations.

During the time that Noble Brewing was finalizing details on that first space (which would fall through), two additional brewing operations were announced: Old Mill Brew Wërks and Below Grade Brewing.

Old Mill Brew Wërks was conceived as a brewpub by co-owners David Love and Lorren Lancaster (the same Lancaster who had been brewing with Silver Moon the year before), with plans to open the pub and restaurant first by October 2010 and the brewery to follow sometime in 2011. The pub would be located on the edge of the Old Mill District and was planning to offer "uncommon" beers not often found in Central Oregon; on the brewery side, Lancaster told the *Bulletin* that they had "plans to make beers that may not be brewed elsewhere in Bend. That includes a few Belgian-style beers, like lambics, and multiple lagers." Plans for the brewery included a fifteen-barrel system and a possible location on Northeast First Street in Bend.

The pub would be open by October, with a dozen taps serving a variety of craft beers, but Lancaster—and the brewery plans—would barely last the rest of the year. By January 2011, Lancaster had departed the venture. In his place stepped another partner in the business, Justin James, who would oversee the brewing of the first beers to carry the Brew Wërks name (beers that would, in fact, be entirely contract-brewed by Silver Moon until 2012).

Below Grade Brewing represented a growing movement that was taking place in the craft beer scene, particularly in Oregon: the establishment of so-called nanobreweries, very small-batch breweries started often by homebrewers who wanted to go pro but were limited by resources and/or experience. A typical brewing capacity would be one barrel (thirty-one gallons) or less, yielding an average yearly output of about one hundred barrels. For the most part, nanobreweries were treated as a steppingstone, a low barrier to entry into the brewing industry, with owners planning to grow into larger operations.

Silver Moon had been the region's original "nanobrewery," although Tyler Reichert had originally conceived of the one-barrel operation as a brew-on-premise addition to his homebrew retail shop. Below Grade's owner Dean Wise was very much fitting the mold of the nano trend. As the *Bulletin* noted in 2010:

> *Dean Wise has applied for a brewery-public house permit from the Oregon Liquor Control Commission, as well as required federal permits, under the name Below Grade Brewing. Wise's plan is to keep Below Grade small as he tests the market "to see if people will buy it on a regular basis—to see if it's worthy."*
>
> *Wise has been a home brewer for 18 years.*
>
> *Initially, Wise plans to brew in his NorthWest Crossing home. For the first six to 12 months, he plans to brew three or four batches of beer at a time, bottling the product for retail sale and possibly selling kegs to bars.*

Wise installed his one-barrel brewery in the basement of his home in the NorthWest Crossing neighborhood on the west side of Bend. He sold his first beers in July 2011.

As 2011 dawned, 10 Barrel Brewing would continue to lead the way forward for this new wave of breweries, with the announcement of two surprising hires: Deschutes Brewery's Jimmy Seifrit and Bend Brewing's Tonya Cornett. Seifrit had been one of the last of the "Old Guard" brewers at Deschutes, having been there since the mid-1990s and (particularly working with brewmaster Larry Sidor) had an influential hand at Deschutes over the previous decade. He had been instrumental in helping to develop the brewery's line of Reserve Series beers and was also the first Deschutes brewer to intentionally sour a beer ("I took a beer I made, Diablo Rim, which was kind of a train wreck of a beer; I played with cardamom, bitter coriander, maybe some orange peel—it kind of tasted a little bit potpourri," said Seifrit. "So I thought one great way to [go] was take this beer, add some [*Brettanomyces*] *bruxellensis* to it, let it go, then add some cherries and raspberries."). This was the inspiration for The Dissident, Deschutes' first commercially released sour ale. 10 Barrel hired Seifrit to help take its brewing operations to that next level of production—building out and expanding into a fifty-barrel brewery.

Cornett had been innovating a number of sour and experimental beers at Bend Brewing over the past several years, experience and knowledge that 10

Barrel desired to run its planned R&D department. With Cornett leaving for the larger brewery, her assistant brewer at Bend Brewing, Ian Larkin, would step into the head brewer role.

In August, 10 Barrel broke ground on its new fifty-barrel brewery on a piece of industrial land in northeast Bend less than one mile from its old location (which still housed the ten-barrel brewery until the new facility was up and running). The groundbreaking ceremony included Jimmy Seifrit smashing open a barrel of beer with a sledgehammer.

Seifrit wouldn't be the only brewer to depart Deschutes that year. Paul Arney and, notably, brewmaster Larry Sidor also announced their departures, both with the intent to start up their own breweries. Arney left in April to pursue a dream of brewing artisanal, small-batch beers, with a concept to "combine age-old techniques alongside modern ones." His beers would be characterized by being entirely fermented and aged in wood and infused with wild yeasts and bacteria native to the national forest surrounding his brewery (which was also his home: he converted his garage into the one-barrel brewery).

Sidor announced his plans to leave in June but would stay with Deschutes through the end of the year. Sidor had long wanted to own his own brewery

Above: GoodLife Brewing features a thirty-barrel brewhouse and canning line. Seen here is the grain mill. *Author's collection.*

Opposite: Jimmy Seifrit breaking open a barrel at the groundbreaking for 10 Barrel's new production brewery. *Author's collection.*

and had been collecting equipment since his days at Olympia Brewing. After eight years at Deschutes Brewery, he felt that the timing was right and had lined up partners Paul Evers of TBD Advertising (an agency handling branding for Deschutes, as well as for 21st Amendment Brewery in California and for Odell Brewing in Colorado) and Dave Wilson (who was working sales at 21st Amendment and had also worked for Deschutes). Through much of the rest of 2011, they would be seeking a location as well as devising a name; in the interim, the alias "856 Brewing" was used (which was TBD's address on Bond Street in downtown Bend).

Noble Brewing was open by June 2011 with a new name: GoodLife Brewing. The name change resulted from a conflict with the newly opened Noble Ale Works in California; although the Central Oregon brewery had applied for a federal trademark on the "Noble" name, Noble Ale Works was operational and brewing beer ahead of it. Rather than dealing with a possible legal battle, it sold the trademark to Noble Ale Works and came up with a new name: GoodLife, reflecting its working motto ("Good beer for the good life") and which it ultimately felt fit its image and lifestyle better than "Noble."

Its location was a cavernous space housing its thirty-barrel brewhouse and several fermenters and offered up plenty of room for future expansion. Renovations had included the addition of the Bierhall, nominally a taproom with a small kitchen that featured communal table seating, and a quarter-acre lawn adjacent to the building that it planned to use as a beer garden. It had two of its own beers available—Mountain Rescue Pale Ale and Sweet As, a pale wheat ale—and filled out the rest of its taps with guest beers.

The debut of Below Grade Brewing came shortly thereafter, during the first weekend of July. Rather than a tasting room or even selling kegs to local bars, owner and brewer Dean Wise and his wife sold the beer at the NorthWest Crossing farmers' market, which took place in the west Bend neighborhood in which they lived, every weekend during the summer. The three beers they served were a South German Hefeweizen, an Old Ale and a Double IPA. By the late fall of that year, these three would be in twenty-two-ounce bottles and sold at the boutique Newport Avenue Market (dubbed Volksvitzen, Old School Ale and Validation Imperial IPA, respectively).

While Old Mill Brew Wërks had been serving beers branded under its own name since the beginning of the year, all the brewing was being contracted out to Silver Moon and would be through the beginning of 2012. It wouldn't be until February 2012 that the Brew Wërks owners would sell the pub portion of the business to focus exclusively on the brewing end: they had lined up a

GoodLife Brewing Company's thirty-barrel brewhouse. *Author's collection.*

location (the space occupied by 10 Barrel's original brewery) and a brewer, Michael McMahon from Langley Brewing in Langley, Washington. They would have the brewery running and be brewing beer later that year.

Outside Bend, the craft beer scene was growing as well (albeit not as quickly as in Bend). In May 2011, it was announced that the city of Prineville would be hosting its first brewery since 1906: Solstice Brewing Company. As reported in Prineville's newspaper, the *Central Oregonian*:

> *Later this year, former Portland resident and long-time homebrewer Joe Barker will open Solstice Brewing Company in the heart of Prineville. Barker grew up in La Grande, Ore., eventually moving to Portland during his college years. He stayed in the city, doing custom woodworking until the recession prompted him to do something new—eventually steering him to Crook County.*
>
> *"I've been brewing probably for 10 years," Barker said. "What really pushed me (to open a brewery) is I've always really enjoyed making craft beer and then having friends over for dinner and just being able to share."*

> *Solstice Brewing Company will occupy the former Main Street Saloon facility, doing business within a block of Pine Theater and the Bowman Museum. Barker hopes to open for business by July—but the beer will have to wait a bit longer.*
>
> *"We probably won't be able to brew beer for several months," he said. "The (Oregon Liquor Control Commission) licensing takes quite a while to get the manufacturing piece."*

In fact, it would be more than a year before Solstice brewed its first beer, in November 2012. That didn't stop the restaurant and pub portion of the business from opening in October 2011.

In Redmond, a new brewery had been quietly setting up shop for about a year and made its brewing debut in 2011: Phat Matt's Brewing. Owner (and former restaurateur) Matt Mulder's goal was to open a production brewery that would produce beer under the Phat Matt's label, as well as offer contract-brewing services to other potential startup breweries. The beer was brewed by Josh Riggs (formerly of Mt. Shasta Brewing Company in Weed, California) on a five-barrel system that was on loan from Larry Johnson, the longtime Bend resident and homebrewer who had owned the Home Brewer in the late '90s. Johnson had been wanting to break into the brewing industry on a professional level; in 2010, he bought the original five-barrel brewing system from Boneyard Brewing and struck an agreement with Mulder to use the system in exchange for help getting Johnson up and running as well. Johnson's company name was to be Shade Tree Brewing, under which he would debut several beers in 2012 (which were in essence contract-brewed at the Phat Matt's brewery).

Phat Matt's debuted with two beers in August, Golden and IPA, with a Red Ale available by November. This debut marked the twelfth brewery opening for Central Oregon (with Bend alone supporting nine of those), and although this would prompt a fresh round of speculation as to whether the market was becoming oversaturated, the industry didn't seem to notice. In addition to the well-publicized plans of Paul Arney and Larry Sidor and the plans for Solstice Brewing by Joe Barker in Prineville, two other brewery projects had been announced in 2011: Rat Hole Brewing, a venture by homebrewer Al Toepfer and his fiancée, Susan McIntosh, on ten acres of rural residential land southeast of Bend, and Worthy Brewing, a planned thirty-barrel production brewery and restaurant located on Bend's east side, headed up by Chad Kennedy, former head brewer at Portland's Laurelwood Brewing Company, and financed by Roger Worthington, lawyer and owner of Indie Hops (a hop broker established in 2009).

Solstice Brewing Company, Prineville's first brewery since 1906. *Author's collection.*

In September 2011, the Brew Shop moved from its location on Division Street to a new, larger building in the heart of Bend, a former church/restaurant that would house the retail portion of the homebrew and bottle shop on the main level and a pub in the basement. Named the Platypus Pub, it would offer more than a dozen taps of craft beer, as well as pub fare from the kitchen, in a comfortable speakeasy-like setting. More pointedly, the owners had also suggested the possibility of setting up their own small in-house brewery, beers from which would be exclusively served in-house.

The Bend beer scene was showing no signs of slowing, and 2012 dawned to an explosion of brewery and brewpub openings that would see nearly as many operations opening in a single year as had opened since 2004. This upward trend would also help to highlight the growth of beer tourism for the region as well, a movement that tapped into Central Oregon's long history of recreation and tourism and, at the same time, helped to create a new economic pillar.

CHAPTER 7

THE BREWERY EXPLOSION AND THE RISE OF BEER TOURISM

At the start of 2012, Bend was still slowly recovering from the Great Recession and the implosion of the housing market; unemployment was in double digits, many property owners were underwater on their real estate investments and the construction that had propped up the economy at the beginning of the century was gone. At the same time, smaller tech companies and startups were creating new jobs, tourism was rising from a 2009 drop and employment in the healthcare industry was climbing. The one industry that had been relatively untouched—indeed, had even grown—was craft beer, and in conjunction with the growing ancillary business of beer tourism, beer was becoming a major component of the regional economy.

Surveys for the summer of 2012 revealed that 7 percent of visitors came to Central Oregon specifically for brewery tourism, and fully 40 percent of all visitors reported brewery visits as part of their activities, up from 28 percent three years earlier. The Bend Ale Trail, established in 2010 by Visit Bend (the tourism-promotion agency for the city), was undoubtedly a factor in this growth. The Bend Ale Trail served as a self-guided tour by which participants collected stamps from each brewery on a foldout map; acquiring all the stamps qualified them for a special prize from the visitor center. The agency estimated that more than four hundred people completed the tour in the first two months.

When it launched in 2010, the Ale Trail included all seven breweries in Bend (Cascade Lakes Brewing's west Bend Lodge, though not outfitted with a brewery itself, was included), as well as Three Creeks in Sisters as an "extra credit" stop. By the end of 2011, GoodLife Brewing and Old Mill Brew Wërks had been added, and an estimated 2,500 people had completed it. As a promotional campaign highlighting the region's beer culture, it proved markedly successful—even so, it would be overshadowed by the rapid increase in the number of brewing operations that the start of 2012 would bring.

At the start of that year, Central Oregon had twelve brewing companies, with nine of those in Bend proper. By the latter half of February, the Ale Apothecary had increased that number to thirteen. Former Deschutes brewer Paul Arney had his "new old world" mountain brewery operational, and the first bottles of his flagship beer, Sahalie, were available for sale by June. Because the output was so limited (Arney brewed one barrel at a time, and the entirely wood-based fermentation and conditioning stages required a longer time to complete), a primary outlet for the beer was an "ale club" that provided three special-release bottles to subscribers each quarter. Other bottles would be released on a limited basis to a few retail shops in Bend and eventually Portland.

Larry Sidor and his partners had secured a location for their yet-to-be-named brewery in a former AAMCO transmission shop in the industrial zone on the edge of the Old Mill District. The renovation and build-out was well underway in early 2012, and in March, they revealed the name of the new brewery: Crux Fermentation Project. A ten-hectoliter (approximately 8.5-barrel) Japanese brewhouse was installed, and Sidor planned to brew a wide variety of beers, ranging from strong ales and styles employing barrel-aging and wild yeasts to lighter styles such as pilsner, Hefeweizen and pale ale. On June 24, Sidor inaugurated the brewery with the very first batch of beer, a Northwest-style pale ale dubbed Just in Time, and Crux was in business that week for a soft opening, with a grand opening event on the thirtieth. (That first beer would not be on tap until almost two weeks after they opened.)

By the time Crux Fermentation Project would open, there would already be another four brewing operations either announced or already in development. Solstice Brewing in Prineville had opened as a pub in October 2011 and was expecting to install brewing equipment later in 2012. Rat Hole Brewing, a small rural venture from Al Toepfer and Susan McIntosh, had been announced in September 2011 and would quietly materialize in 2013. In February 2012, the Sunriver Brewing Company was announced, the first-ever brewpub to be established in the resort town of Sunriver, south of Bend. Although plans originally called for a small (three-barrel) in-house brewery, that would not come to fruition; when the brewpub opened that July, the beers were contract-brewed by Phat Matt's Brewing out of Redmond.

Barrels of conditioning beer take up much of the limited space at the Ale Apothecary. *Author's collection.*

Crux Fermentation Project, located in what was once an AAMCO transmission garage. *Author's collection.*

But by far the largest of the up-and-coming breweries was Worthy Brewing, a planned thirty-barrel production brewery and beer garden that would be located on nearly three acres of land on the eastern edge of Bend. The principal behind Worthy was Roger Worthington, a part-time Bend resident and attorney who made his fortune specializing in asbestos litigation. In 2009, he partnered with longtime friend Jim Solberg to start Indie Hops, a hop broker representing Willamette Valley hops, with a particular focus on research and breeding. Worthington owned the land for the proposed brewery, and in the spring of 2011, he began discussions with the City of Bend to explore the possibility of his brewery idea.

The project moved forward, and by June, brewer Chad Kennedy had come on board. Kennedy had been brewing at Laurelwood Brewing in Portland since 2003 and took over the brewmaster role in 2006 when Christian Ettinger left to start Hopworks Urban Brewery. Before joining the brewery, Kennedy had been an avid homebrewer and had been working for Portland beer distributor Aria Imports to get his foot in the door in the industry. During his time at Laurelwood, he had built an impressive brewing résumé, including the introduction of the popular Workhorse IPA, as well as the brewery's first Belgian-style sour ales.

Worthy Brewing was officially announced in July, and in February 2012, it conducted the official groundbreaking ceremony to much fanfare. Construction progressed quickly throughout the year, and Kennedy and head brewer Dustin Kellner (also from Laurelwood) brewed the first test batch of beer in mid-December. The brewery would officially open for business with a soft launch in February 2013.

The news may have been abuzz with the new breweries, but the established ones were keeping pace. Deschutes Brewery's downtown Public House had been undergoing a yearlong expansion throughout most of 2011 and closed entirely for the month of January 2012 to finish the remodel. This expansion added a second level and more than doubled the seating capacity, including a special event space. The production brewery was also undergoing expansion throughout 2012 that would increase the brewery's annual capacity by 105,000 barrels.

At Silver Moon Brewing, head brewer Tyler West announced his departure in February 2012. He had accepted a brewing position at Oakshire Brewing in Eugene, and in his place, brewer Brett Thomas stepped into the head brewer role.

By the start of the year, 10 Barrel Brewing had completed construction on its new fifty-barrel brewery and was brewing beer. It also announced

Roger Worthington and Chad Kennedy at the groundbreaking for Worthy Brewing. *Author's collection.*

Deschutes Brewery's expanded Public House, downtown Bend. *Courtesy Deschutes Brewery.*

another high-profile brewer hire in Shawn Kelso, the longtime brewer at Barley Brown's Brewpub in Baker City, Oregon. Kelso would work on product development with Jimmy Seifrit and Tonya Cornett and would head up the brewery's new Boise, Idaho brewpub.

Boneyard Brewing was experiencing explosive growth, due in large part to its hugely popular RPM IPA, brewing about 1,300 barrels of beer its first year (2010); that number increased to nearly 10,000 barrels for 2012. Demand for its beer was huge, so much so that it was forced to constantly expand its capacity just to keep up with its draft accounts; it also continued to put off plans to can its beer. (Its plan for canning had been announced early on, and it even had a $35,000 canning line sitting idle.) At the beginning of 2012, it signed a lease on a new building in northeast Bend that would house a new fifty-barrel brewery, although build-out would be slow over the next two years as the brewery struggled just to keep up with demand for its beer.

That summer of 2012 was a busy one for Central Oregon's new brewing operations. Crux Fermentation Project opened at the end of June, and although its first beer wouldn't be on tap until almost two weeks after opening, Larry Sidor was brewing prolifically. By early August, it would be offering five of its own beers along with an extensive guest taplist. Construction on Worthy Brewing was underway, and brewer Chad Kennedy teamed up with GoodLife Brewing to brew a collaboration beer dubbed The Good and Worthy (which could perhaps be considered Worthy's first beer). Larry Johnson had been working with Phat Matt's to produce the first of his Shade Tree beers, which he debuted at the Old Mill District's inaugural Fermentation Celebration in mid-July.

Sunriver Brewing opened its doors on July 4, with a lineup of four beers that had been brewed at Phat Matt's: a pale ale (brewed from a recipe developed by owner Brian Cameron), an amber, an IPA and a stout. The pub was located in the Village at Sunriver, the heart of the resort community's retail shopping and dining district, and although the beers were being contract-brewed in Redmond, the owners were anxious to bring the beer production in-house and establish their own brewery.

In August, Solstice Brewing in Prineville acquired brewing equipment and began the installation process. It wouldn't be until late November, however, that Solstice fired up its system and brewed its first batch of beer, Solstice Pale Ale. As it was, it was nearly beaten to the punch by a new brewpub in Redmond that would ultimately be the smallest operation (brewery *or* brewpub) Central Oregon had seen to date: Smith Rock Brewing. The four partners in the venture (Danielle and Kevin Stuart,

Natalie Patterson and Donald Fredrickson) had applied for a brewpub license from the Oregon Liquor Control Commission in April 2012, and by October, they had officially announced their plans to open the small brewpub by November. As reported in the *Bulletin*:

> *Initially, Smith Rock Brewing will rely on a small 25-gallon system to make beer for customers at its Northwest Seventh Street pub, where traditional locally sourced pub fare will also be for sale, said Natalie Patterson, brewmaster and one of four partners in the company.*
>
> *Later, the company would like to increase production and start distributing to restaurants and stores with a larger system off-site, Patterson said. But that doesn't mean people should expect Smith Rock to turn into a large-scale brewer distributing in multiple states.*

The small size of their operation—0.8 barrels—dictated that they would be able to offer only one of their in-house beers on tap at any given time. But by the end of 2012, Smith Rock had joined other Central Oregon outliers Sunriver and Solstice to bring the total count of brewing operations to eighteen (eleven of those in Bend alone).

The Bend Ale Trail was benefitting from this explosive brewery growth, although ironically new breweries and brewpubs were opening more frequently than Visit Bend updated and printed maps. In 2012, the Ale Trail was successful enough to run a contest to win beer for a year and was receiving attention in the national media. But it was merely the most prominent example of the beer tourism that had been developing in the region for the past several years. Central Oregon had, of course, long been known for its outdoor recreational opportunities and quality of life, and the marriage of craft beer to the tourist industry was a natural progression as the number of breweries had grown. The tipping point for this development seemed to occur in about 2004–5.

Outdoor guide company Wanderlust Tours added a special beer tasting to its popular canoe tours in 2005, one of the first companies to explicitly offer beer as a tourist activity in Central Oregon. It offered a similar beer-themed snowshoe excursion that winter; both would become regular packages. The opening of McMenamins Old St. Francis School in the fall of 2004 helped further solidify the idea of Bend as a "beer destination." McMenamins (a destination in itself) offered lodging packages that often featured beer specials, often in conjunction with special events or partners (Wanderlust Tours was one such partner package). And the first-ever Bend Brew Fest took place in

August 2004, featuring beer from twenty breweries, pouring at the Old Mill District's Les Schwab Amphitheater. This was the first festival of its kind in Central Oregon, and its success helped pave the way for additional festivals in subsequent years, including ones such as the Bend Oktoberfest, the Little Woody Barrel-Aged Brew Fest and the Sisters Fresh Hop Festival.

The Ale Trail would inspire the launch of services tapping directly into the beer tourism market: guided beer tours. Wanderlust Tours was again among the first with its Bend Brew Bus, launched in 2010, offering guided tours of local breweries with special tastings and Ale Trail stamps. Others followed suit, offering specialized beer tours—such as the Green Energy Transportation & Intra-Area Tours Shuttle and Bend Adventure Tours—or blending the essence of the region's outdoor recreation lifestyle with beer tours to create unique experiences, such as the pedal-powered Cycle Pub and the horse-drawn Cowboy Carriage.

The opening of new breweries continued to outpace this near-parallel growth in beer tourism, however. Worthy Brewing opened its doors at the beginning of February 2013, featuring an impressive facility that housed not only a thirty-barrel brewhouse and cavernous warehouse space for expansion but also a restaurant, an expansive beer garden, a small hopyard and a greenhouse to grow its own herbs and experimental hop varieties. It opened with five house beers (Go Time Xtra Pale Ale, Lights Out Stout, East Side Pale Ale, IPA and Imperial IPA), and plans called for bottling as well as canning beer within the year for wide distribution. (GoodLife Brewing would actually beat it to cans; in March, it canned its first beers, Sweet As and Descender IPA, becoming the first brewery in the region to do so.)

At the other end of the spectrum was Rat Hole Brewing, a nanobrewery operation located southeast of Bend on rural farmland and installed in a renovated barn outbuilding (originally little more than a shed). Owners Al Toepfer and Susan McIntosh had moved from their hometown of Snoqualmie, Washington, in 2010 to try their hand at opening a brewery. Toepfer had been an automotive technician for more than three decades and had been homebrewing for a number of years, garnering awards for his beers along the way. McIntosh was an accountant and worked as the corporate controller for Bellevue, Washington–based Woodmark Retirement Corporation. They found their way to Central Oregon when McIntosh's brother, Les Keele, offered the outbuilding on his ten acres of land as a possible brewery location.

Rat Hole Brewing was originally announced in 2011, but owners Toepfer and McIntosh (who were married in 2012) had kept a low profile as work

Worthy Brewing Company's expansive production facility includes a restaurant and a beer garden. *Author's collection.*

was underway on the brewery, in large part because "we've been working on trying to get our beer at a level we thought was worthy of public distribution," as Susan Toepfer told the *Bulletin* in February 2013. That was the month their first beers had become public, as they had started sending out samples to pubs and growler fill stations to test the market. Those first beers were Harvester Red Ale and Fence Post Porter, flagships of a larger line that Al Toepfer was steadily brewing on the 2.5-barrel system they had installed.

Although their main goal was to open a brewpub, the Toepfers initially sold their beer in bottles and on draft at several locations in Bend and even in their hometown of Snoqualmie. However, it would not be long before they found the ideal location for their brewpub. In May, Old Mill Brew Wërks moved its brewpub restaurant from the small space on the eastern edge of the Old Mill District to a much larger space overlooking the Deschutes River a half mile away. The vacated space was already configured with a kitchen and bar, and it was already known as a brewpub (the not-yet-updated Bend Ale Trail maps still listed Old Mill Brew Wërks at that location), so the Toepfers jumped on the opportunity the location presented. The Rat Hole

Brewpub opened on July 16, 2013, serving up Southwest-style cuisine and becoming the sole outlet for the Rat Hole lineup of beers. It would be added to the Bend Ale Trail map the following year.

There were big changes in the works for Silver Moon Brewing during this time. In May 2013, head brewer Brett Thomas announced that he was leaving Silver Moon to take the head brewer position with Sunriver Brewing. The owners at Sunriver had been eager to move away from having their beers contract-brewed and open their own production facility; as such, a deciding factor for Thomas taking the position was the challenge and opportunity to build a brewery from the ground up. That wasn't the only change for Silver Moon, however; in July, it was revealed that Tyler Reichert had sold the brewery. The new owners were James Watts, who had founded the Cycle Pub in 2010, and Matt Barrett, who owned two of the three Bend Snap Fitness centers.

Watts and Barrett wanted to focus on increasing production and distribution, as well as bring a fresh identity and awareness to the brewing company. Part of that effort would be in making over the downtown brewpub, retaining the elements that had defined the location (such as the vibrant live music scene and intimate pub space) while replacing or removing other elements entirely (such as the pool table and the bar top). The efforts paid off: the brewery brewed a record 1,400 barrels of beer for 2013 and was on track to brew at least 1,600 for 2014. It had signed with Columbia Distributing in the spring of 2014 to consolidate all of its distribution for Oregon and Washington.

The rest of 2013 would be occupied with the news—and openings—of a number of new, small breweries, bringing the total count to twenty-four for Central Oregon by the year's end. The news broke in August about the slew of new operations: Oblivion Brewing, North Rim Brewing, Bridge 99 Brewery, Juniper Brewing and RiverBend Brewing. Of these, Juniper Brewing (located in Redmond) and North Rim Brewing wouldn't be open and active until 2014.

Oblivion was the first to hit the market with its beer, with a release party in late August featuring three beers: Backside IPA, Polar Star Pale Ale and Knock Out Stout. (This release was held at a local beer bar, as Oblivion was strictly production with no tasting room space.) Owner and brewer Darin Butschy had previously brewed for SLO Brewing in Paso Robles, California, and then for Firestone Walker Brewing when the latter bought SLO. The beers were initially brewed on a half-barrel system (fifteen gallons), the smallest commercial brewery the region had yet seen, but in February 2014, Oblivion acquired a ten-barrel system.

The next operation to go live was Bridge 99 Brewery, in September. Owner Trever Hawman had been a homebrewer for six years before building his 1.5-barrel brewing system in a converted space behind his home in Bend. He had struck a deal with a local restaurant, Wubba's BBQ Shack, to be the primary outlet to serve his beers, starting with Candle Creek Ale (a pale ale), ISA (an India session ale) and India pale ale.

It was Bridge 99 that helped the Platypus Pub with the first of several beers under its own label. The first beer, Arch Rival IPA, was brewed that September to be on tap for an October reopening of the Pub after several weeks of renovations. These would be followed up with Haste Ye Back (a Wee Heavy) and Flat Tail Pale Ale.

RiverBend Brewing was pouring beer by the end of October from its location on the north-central side of Bend. Formerly Rivals Sport Bar, owner Gary Sobala wanted to shed the Texas hold 'em tournaments that Rivals was known for and instead add a brewpub component. Accordingly, he installed a ten-barrel brewing system in a separate building on the property and hired brewer Dan Olsen to craft the beers. Olsen came from 10 Barrel Brewing (and Deschutes Brewery before that), and he planned to first brew traditional beers before beginning to "experiment with herbs, fruits and spices," as he told the *Bulletin*. The first two beers from the new brewpub debuted in late October: RiverBend IPA and Blonde Ale.

RiverBend would be the final brewery opening for 2013 (finishing the year representing the twenty-fourth brewing operation for Central Oregon), but the next year would find Sunriver Brewing's new production facility up and running, and three new breweries nipping at its heels.

Sunriver's facility was a fifteen-barrel brewery, the build-out of which had been overseen by head brewer Brett Thomas. On January 1, Thomas brewed the first beer on the new system: Chalk Rock Amber Ale. Thomas quickly followed up with Baselayer Black Ale, Shred Head Winter Ale and Vicious Mosquito IPA. A three-barrel pilot brewing system was installed and operational by the spring.

The first of the new breweries was Juniper Brewing (located in Redmond), a two-barrel production brewing operation (with a tasting room) launched by homebrewers Curtis Endicott and Scott Lesmeister. They celebrated their opening with a ribbon cutting in March featuring three beers at launch: Old Roy IPA, Jolly Black Ale and the Milk Man (a Belgian-style white ale).

Wild Ride Brewing was next, also located in Redmond. Owner Brian Mitchell had ambitious plans and located the production brewery in a former Parr Lumber warehouse in Redmond's revitalized downtown district, which offered up 8,700 square feet of space to house a twenty-barrel brewery and plenty of fermenters. Mitchell hired as the head brewer Paul Bergeman, who had previously brewed at Laurelwood Brewing in Portland and Kona Brewing in Hawaii. Wild Ride celebrated its official opening on May 10, offering up nine beers on tap.

And finally, the region's twenty-seventh brewery (and Bend's eighteenth), North Rim Brewing, began selling beer shortly after Wild Ride opened. Owner Shane Neilsen and his partners, who had been homebrewing for years, had been working on the brewery for more than a year, and it had been announced as "coming soon" as early as August 2013. The brewery featured a ten-barrel brewhouse with three thirty-barrel fermenters, with three flagship beers sold on draft and in bottles: SingleTrack IPA, Roundabout Stout and Skyline Belgian Pale Ale.

Unfortunately, even with more than two dozen breweries proving Bend and Central Oregon a thriving market for craft beer, there would inevitably be casualties. As of this writing, Phat Matt's Brewing of Redmond is out of business. Larry Johnson has been reorganizing his Shade Tree Brewing to turn his five-barrel brewing system (the one he had originally purchased from Boneyard and that was in use at Phat Matt's) into a small production brewery on his property southwest of Bend, and he is still building out the necessary infrastructure to set up the brewery.

CHAPTER 8

BEER TOWN, USA

In 2008, Charlie Papazian, author of *The Complete Joy of Homebrewing* as well as founder of the Association of Brewers and the Great American Beer Festival, wrote an article for his Examiner.com column attempting to determine what city held the honors as "Beertown, USA." Bend placed number six on that list (determined as a per capita number of breweries for cities with three or more), with six breweries giving an estimated count of one brewery for every 12,427 people.

In 2014, with eighteen breweries and an estimated population of 81,236 (based on 2013 estimates), the per capita count has dropped to one brewery for every 4,513 people. Bend and Central Oregon not only have a thriving market for craft beer but also enjoy a vibrant beer culture, one that has helped support the development of a strong regional "beer economy" that has spun out from the brewing scene to include incidental activities and business opportunities.

Beer tourism is the primary and most visible of these ancillary activities, a natural evolution of the region's history and dependence on tourism and recreation. Of course, beer has long accompanied enthusiasts on their outdoor excursions, be they camping, fishing, skiing on the mountain, trips to the lake and so on. As recounted in the previous chapter, in Central Oregon the outdoor guide company Wanderlust Tours was among the first to explicitly link craft beer with the regional tourist industry, offering specialty beer tasting as a feature of several excursions. With the creation of the Bend Ale Trail by Visit Bend in 2010, several companies began offering customized "beer tours" that supplemented the Ale Trail and highlighted the region's melding of craft beer culture with the local lifestyle. The Cycle Pub stands out as a perfect example.

The Cycle Pub was the brainchild of James Watts, a software entrepreneur from Danville, California, who had come to Bend in 2008. (This was the same Watts who, along with Matt Barrett, purchased Silver Moon Brewing in 2013.) Watts had first been exposed to the concept while visiting Cologne, Germany, where he had seen a similar device in operation: the BierBike. For all intents and purposes, it was a pub on wheels powered by human pedalers, and Watts decided it would be a natural fit for Bend ("I knew in my gut that the beer factor, the bike factor and kind of the liberal, try-anything-once nature of Bend was just a good fit," said Watts). In 2010, he began looking into importing a BierBike for the local market. However, he saw an opportunity to build an American version locally and turned to Atek Customs in September 2010 to build the first Cycle Pub. It was completed just in time to debut at the Bend WinterFest on February 18, 2011.

Although the current riding experience adheres to a bring-your-own-beer model, the original Cycle Pub, as its name would suggest, did have the ability to pour beer. However, there turned out to be a fatal flaw, as Watts recounted in an interview:

> *The original bike has a large, two-head tower, one of which was wired to a pump and a water tank, just to help keep people hydrated in the summer months. And the other was intended for a keg. So we did have a couple of outings in the April–May* [2011] *timeframe, including…one of the guys who at the time was a bartender at 10 Barrel; he brought a sixth-barrel onto the bike for a group of him and his friends* [who] *were going out. And one thing that we hadn't thought about was, bouncing around town, how foamy a keg would get. And as skilled as this guy was with a good pour and tapping a keg, it was a disaster. We gave it one more shot after that, and just because it was a mess, and it was foamy, and people were disappointed, we decided almost immediately no more kegs on the bike.*

The Cycle Pub ultimately proved successful, though, and Watts received requests to build the specialty bike for other cities. As a result, he split the manufacturing part of the business off from the touring business and built and licensed Cycle Pubs for other cities, including Boise, Idaho; Las Vegas; and Traverse City, Michigan. His Bend fleet expanded as well to include two of the larger pub bikes, two smaller "conference" bikes that seat six and a small shuttle. Watts estimated that the Cycle Pub has accommodated about twelve thousand riders in the first three years of the business.

The concept of the multi-rider party bike was not new, but the Cycle Pub was among the first in the country to incorporate the "pub" concept and allow riders to consume beer while pedaling—thanks in large part to the leeway in licensing afforded by the City of Bend and the Oregon Liquor Control Commission (OLCC).

The Cycle Pub was not the only "first" that Bend had to offer the beer community. In 2012, the Growler Guys, the first dedicated growler fill station in Oregon, opened, kicking off a wave of similar businesses that would grow rapidly across the state.

Growlers, glass or ceramic jugs used to transport draft beer, have a long history in American beer, dating to the late nineteenth and early twentieth centuries, when people would fill small galvanized pails with fresh beer from their local pubs to take home. According to lore, the name "growler" possibly comes from the rumbling sound made by the lid of the pail as carbon dioxide escaped. In 1989, Wyoming's Otto Brothers' Brewing Company claimed introduction of the modern sixty-four-ounce glass growler by founders Charlie and Ernie Otto. (Otto Brothers' relocated to Victor, Idaho, in 1998 and changed its name to Grand Teton Brewing in 2000.)

The Growler Guys was started by Kent Couch along with his son, Kizer, who owned the Shell Stop and Go gas station and convenience store on the east side of Bend. Located on a busy intersection on the way into and out of town, the store offered a better-than-average selection of craft beer and, by some accounts, was one of the busiest convenience store beer retailers in the state. The Couches, always on the lookout for ways to improve their offerings, read about standalone growler fill stations being established on the East Coast and saw no reason why such a venture shouldn't be wildly successful in Bend. They ran into one, however: OLCC licensing regulations did not allow it.

More specifically, the OLCC did not know *how* to determine licensing requirements for a growler fill station. Breweries and brewpubs had long filled growlers of beer to go, of course; their licensing allowed such sales of beer for off-premise consumption. And retailers could be licensed with off-premise permits to sell packaged beer. A combination of the two had not been considered before, although eventually the OLCC allowed the Couches to open their growler station (requiring an additional liquor license to do so). The Growler Guys opened in March 2012 with a twelve-tap fill station, and by the end of the year, it had expanded to thirty taps.

It was successful from the start, and this success inspired rapid opening and growth of other growler stations, such as Gorilla Growlers (located inside the Empire Car Wash building in north Bend), Growler Phil's (sharing space on Bend's west side with Primal Cuts meat market) and Beer Dawgs in Redmond. In Sunriver, Mark Cornett (husband of Tonya Cornett) opened up The Mountain Jug, a beer bar and bottle shop that also focused on growlers. Other growler fill businesses opened up elsewhere in Oregon as well. For Growler Guys, the model was successful and popular enough that it opened a second location on Bend's west side and turned the business into a franchise operation, with additional Growler Guys franchises in Eugene, Portland and Astoria, Oregon, as well as Richland and Spokane, Washington (as of this writing, two additional locations are slated to open in Boise, Idaho, and Tualatin, Oregon).

The growing popularity of the growler fill stations helped to inspire growth in the growler business itself, particularly in the manufacture of new types of growlers beyond the traditional glass bottle. Hydro Flask—a company founded in Bend in 2008 that manufactures vacuum-insulated, stainless steel bottles in various sizes—was among the first to release a specialty stainless steel insulated growler. Another Bend company, Drink Tanks, was originally founded in 2010 and released a similar insulated growler that could include an optional lid attachment mimicking the tap apparatus of a beer keg. Both of these products and others blend well with the recreational lifestyle that Central Oregon has to offer.

When it comes to combining beer culture with recreation, few beer-related products are as complementary as the Silipint. Launched in 2010, the Silipint was the invention of Rick Fredland, who had originally created a collapsible dog bowl using food-grade silicone. (This was also popular in Bend, which has long been a very dog-friendly town.) Fredland applied the same idea to a beer pint glass design, resulting in an unbreakable, flexible (though not entirely collapsible or foldable) drinking glass that proved highly popular with the outdoor lifestyle. That popularity allowed the company to offer smaller versions and even a shot glass (that doubles as a golf tee). This popularity received an additional boost from the Bend Ale Trail, as a commemorative Silipint is awarded as the prize to those who complete the trail.

Not all beer is consumed on a Cycle Pub or from a Silipint poured from a growler on a trail halfway up a mountain. In 2014, nearly every restaurant, tavern and bar in Bend has a variety of craft beer available on tap, and there are two beer bars that focus almost exclusively on craft. Before Deschutes Brewery was established in 1988, however, most beer sold was Budweiser,

Worthy Brewing's first seasonal winter ale, Powder Keg. *Author's collection.*

Coors, Blitz-Weinhard and similar pale lagers. A few downtown Bend bars, such as Player's Grille and McKenzie's, served "micros" that were prevalent at the time (Sierra Nevada, Widmer, BridgePort, Pyramid and the like). The presence of craft beer on tap grew over the years, but it wasn't until the 2000s that establishments began to expand and focus on their beer selection with an eye toward drawing customers in for the beer itself. In 2007, the Blacksmith Restaurant (located in a former blacksmith shop started by Joe Egg in 1923) underwent renovation and reopened with twelve taps dedicated to a selection of craft and import beers.

In 2009, Bend's first true beer bar, the Abbey Pub, was opened by Geoff Marlowe, a homebrewer active with the local Central Oregon Homebrewers Organization. Inspired by the Bier Stein in Eugene, Marlowe wanted to bring that concept to Bend—twelve rotating taps of beer along with a bottle selection of at least 150 more that patrons could purchase and open on premise. The Abbey Pub was moderately successful, although Marlowe ultimately was not able to maintain the grueling schedule; although he had hired some evening help, he ran much of the pub himself six days a week, from eleven o'clock in the morning until ten o'clock in the evening. In 2011, he sold the pub.

The purchasers were Jason and Jennifer Powell, Andy Polanchek and Diana Fischetti, who wanted to maintain the beer bar concept but set about expanding the kitchen and the overall footprint of the space. In early February 2012, they officially opened the Broken Top Bottle Shop & Ale Café, and shortly thereafter, they expanded into the adjacent space in the building (a former wine bar). The expanded space accommodated a large bank of coolers for their bottled beer offerings, as well as room to host events. Since its opening, the revamped beer bar has enjoyed considerable success and popularity; it's known both for its impressive beer selection and the quality of the food, becoming one of the area's premier beer destinations.

This distinction is shared by the Platypus Pub, the beer bar located beneath the Brew Shop homebrew supply store that opened in the latter half of 2011, when the Brew Shop moved from its former location on Division Street. The pub occupies the basement space below the Brew Shop, offering fifteen taps of beer, as well as the full selection of the homebrew shop's bottled beer upstairs. Like Broken Top Bottle Shop, the Platypus Pub hosts events such as beer tastings and even small-scale festivals and homebrew events.

Outside of the beer bars, the number of beer festivals and special events in Central Oregon has grown along with the increase in the number of breweries, although it was not until the inaugural Bend Brew Fest in 2004 that the concept of beer-as-event solidified locally. Beer had, of course, long been present at events in the form of beer gardens and the like. And Deschutes Brewery in 1989 created the annual charity-driven Sagebrush Classic golf tournament, for which it brewed a specialty beer each year. It was the Bend Brew Fest, however, that bridged the gap, celebrating beer itself rather than treating it as the beverage component to a larger event. Modeled loosely after other outdoor beer festivals, such as Portland's Oregon Brewers Festival, the Brew Fest featured twenty breweries pouring beer samples in open-air tents at the Les Schwab Amphitheater. The festival proved popular and would return each subsequent year (except for 2009); it would serve as the most "mainstream" of the region's festivals, even as it helped open doors for other specialized events.

The Little Woody Barrel-Aged Brew Fest, which debuted in 2009, filled a void left by the absence of that year's Bend Brew Fest (which had run into OLCC licensing issues due to an incident the previous year involving an intoxicated minor and a golf cart joyride). The Little Woody focused entirely on specialty beers aged with wood in some manner (in barrels, on oak spirals and so on) and eschewed the typical type of beerfest venue in favor of a more intimate setting at the Des Chutes Historical Museum. Despite the niche nature of the event, the fest has grown in popularity and attendance each year, becoming one of the region's premier beer events and even spawning an associated festival in Portland dubbed the Big Woody in January 2014.

The Sisters Fresh Hop Festival is another example of a niche event that, like the Little Woody, has grown larger and more popular each subsequent year. The Oregon Brewers Guild and Travel Oregon had been producing a series of "Fresh Hop Tastivals" since 2004 that traveled to several cities across the state, and although they brought the event to Deschutes Brewery in 2007, for the most part Central Oregon was omitted from the "tastival" events. In 2010, Three Creeks Brewing in Sisters spearheaded the organization of a fresh hop beer festival with the Sisters Chamber of Commerce, and that September, the first Sisters Fresh Hop Festival took place in the town's Village Green Park. The festival featured only beers brewed with fresh-picked hops ("fresh" because they are mere hours from the bine and have not been dried), of which there is a proliferation in the Pacific Northwest due to the region being a major hop producer. The first year, the Sisters festival featured ten breweries pouring these unique beers; by 2013, that number had risen to fifteen breweries pouring twenty-two fresh-hop beers (along with a few "standard" beers). According to Three Creeks' Wade Underwood, the 2014 festival will feature between twenty and twenty-four breweries.

Bend is host to a growing number of other events and festivals each year—smaller, niche events highlighting a particular style of beer, specialty beer dinners and even an annual "beer week" celebration. Central Oregon Beer Week (COBW) was launched in May 2012 as a celebration of the region's craft beer culture, and like other beer weeks around the country, it helps to organize and promote a weeklong series of special events. Included in the number of events that COBW helped to launch or promote are the "SMaSH" fest (which stands for "Single Malt and Single Hop," beers brewed with only one of each of these particular ingredients) and the Sunriver Brewfest. (The author is a prominent founder of COBW.)

Examples of other specialty events include a beer festival hosted by the local Whole Foods Market (first taking place in 2011); the Fermentation

Specialty beer brewed for Central Oregon Beer Week 2013; participants who found a gnome were awarded passes to the Little Woody. *Author's collection.*

Celebration in the Old Mill District (started in 2012), offering a "beer walk" throughout the outdoor shopping district and highlighting all local breweries; and numerous small fests hosted by McMenamins Old St. Francis School throughout the year.

All of these events represent a significant contribution to the regional beer economy, particularly as they help to draw in visitors from outside the area. (Many of the bigger events offer special lodging packages with local hotels.) For the summer of 2013, a Bend visitor survey revealed that 45 percent of respondents included brewery visits and/or the Bend Ale Trail among their activities (54 percent reported simply visiting a brewery), with 6 percent reporting brewery tourism specifically as the main purpose of travel to Bend. To help put these percentages in perspective, Dean Runyon Associates reported the annual tourist spending for Deschutes County to be nearly $500 million that same year.

It's not just in tourist dollars that beer feeds the local economy. In 2013, the brewing companies in Central Oregon employed about 870 people (1.32 percent of private-sector employment), up from approximately 450 in 2010. Hundreds if not thousands more were employed by businesses in some way affected by the brewing industry, such as beverage distributors, construction, beer bars, growler fill stations, Silipints and even hop growers.

In the latter category, hops have traditionally been the purview of the more temperate Willamette Valley west of the Cascades, although commercial hop farming in Central Oregon was not unheard of. In the early years of the twentieth century, Bend resident Henry Hedges announced plans to grow a dozen acres of hops on his homestead. In the mid-1940s, the Ochoco Hop ranch produced hops for several years. From the *Bulletin*, September 19, 1946:

> *Residents of Central Oregon were more than surprised early this month when a call for 200 hop pickers was issued from Prineville, for, outside of the Crook county town, few knew that hops are being produced in this part of the state on a commercial scale. The hop yards are just east of Prineville, on Ochoco creek, and are on the Ochoco Hop ranch, managed by Delbert Haener.*
>
> *Hop picking got underway shortly before the first of the month and the work is still in progress.*
>
> *Thirty five acres were in hops on the Ochoco ranch this season, following a fine yield last year.*
>
> *Last year, the green hops were shipped from the Ochoco yards to Independence, where they were dried. This year, a drier was erected at the Prineville yards.*

In 2006, two couples decided to pool their resources on their farms northwest of Bend and start the Tumalo Hops Company. Gary and Susan Wyatt and Roger and Mary Janson planted about three hundred hop plants on a quarter acre of land, with the idea to sell the hops to homebrewers. In 2009, they harvested about forty ounces of hops. In 2010, it was twenty pounds, and by 2012, their yield had reached about eight hundred pounds. The commercial breweries took note; in 2011, 10 Barrel Brewing purchased forty pounds of Tumalo Farms hops, which brewer Tonya Cornett used in a pale ale named Local Joe. By 2014, they were receiving orders for their hops before harvest.

Commercial hop cultivation will never become a prominent industry in Central Oregon as compared to the Willamette Valley or Washington's Yakima Valley, although there is certainly opportunity for small growers such as Tumalo Hops and the Smith Rock Hop Farm (established in 2014). Rather it is one of many factors that contribute to the region's beer culture and economy that have helped propel Bend into the national spotlight—a trend that has also been fueled in part by articles from the *New York Times*, CNN, the *Seattle Times*, the *Washington Post*, the *Boston Globe* and others. In a nod to Charlie Papazian's original 2008 poll, Bend has increasingly become known as "Beer Town, USA."

And no wonder: the industry not only survived the economic crash of the past decade but also managed to thrive, even as Bend's other industries began their slow recovery. Bend is home to the fifth-largest craft brewery in the country, Deschutes Brewery, as well as two of the fastest-growing breweries in Oregon, 10 Barrel Brewing and Boneyard Brewing. (10 Barrel even announced the opening of a new brewpub in Portland as this book was being written.) Beer recreation and beer tourism have become integral activities for nearly half the visitors to Bend (not to mention the year-round residents). This goes beyond just the likes of the Bend Ale Trail and the Cycle Pub—there are beer runs, bicycling pub crawls, canoeing beer excursions, beer golf and more.

Central Oregon does not have the historical brewing background that many of the country's vibrant beer regions enjoy. Yet locals appreciated quality of beer alongside their quality of life long before the craft beer movement began, so it is perhaps not surprising that craft beer has woven itself into the Central Oregon culture so thoroughly. How else to explain the unlikely explosion of breweries in a region isolated from larger population centers and interstate highways? Or that grocery stores hold beer festivals and that you can fill a growler with fresh beer at a gas station or a car wash? Bend even offers a non-alcoholic beer for dogs: Dawg Grog, made from wort (unfermented barley syrup) from Boneyard Brewing.

It is not surprising, but it's not necessarily a given, either. Much credit can be given to Deschutes Brewery, which pioneered the craft beer concept in an isolated, recession-plagued mill town nearly three decades ago. Gary Fish, on the eve of Deschutes Brewery's twenty-sixth anniversary, offered some insight into what makes Deschutes (and, by extension, much of the rest of the craft beer movement) successful:

> We in the craft beer movement tend to make it a lot more about us. "It's my beer, it's my vision, it's my this, it's my that." It's not about us, it's not about the beer, it's about the people [the customers]. It's about the people who we get to work with. And if you can inspire those two groups, you can conquer the world, you can do anything.
>
> You want to know what Deschutes Brewery's about, you come in here at 5:30 just about any night, and you look around, and you see what's happening, and you got people who come in here, they're locals, they're visitors, they're white collar, they're blue collar, they're young, they're old, they're white, they're black, they're male, they're female...What are they doing? They're talking to each other. They're enjoying a beer, they're laughing, they're arguing, they're joking, they're teasing, they're interacting. And I think that's incredibly rare in society these days. And especially in this electronic age we live in. Here, everybody's accountable. Everybody's interested. You can agree, disagree, talk about sports, politics, current events, your family, my family. It doesn't matter. But you're talking.
>
> I'd argue that dynamic...doesn't happen in a wine bar, or in a bar where most drinks are served in a martini glass, in colors not commonly found in nature. But over beer, it's different. And that as much as anything else frames our business going forward into the future. And everything we do is around creating that experience.

Whether past, present or future, one thing is certain: Bend beer *is* about the experience.

TIMELINE

1868   Barney Prine settles in what will become Prineville, establishing the first store, blacksmith shop and saloon.

1877   Farewell Bend Ranch is established by John Y. Todd.

1880   City of Prineville is incorporated by the State of Oregon.

1882   Ochoco Brewery is established in Prineville by Frank Loacker and a partner named Solomon.

1884   Loacker sells the Ochoco Brewery to Asa Miles and Ed Evans.

1888   Ochoco Brewery is destroyed by fire and is rebuilt by Asa Miles.

1890   Ochoco Brewery is closed.

1893   Prineville Brewery in Prineville is opened by George O'Neil.

1894   John Geiger, brewmaster, joins Prineville Brewery.

1903   Bend has two saloons, as noted by the *Bend Bulletin.*

1905   City of Bend is incorporated.

Bend has eight saloons and a "lusty red light district" at the lower end of town.

1906   Prineville Brewery is closed.

1908   Prohibition is established in Crook County under local option.

1910   Local-option prohibition is repealed in Crook County.

1911   The railroad comes to Bend.

1912   Bend has twelve saloons.

1916   Oregon statewide prohibition goes into effect.

Shevlin-Hixon and Brooks-Scanlon sawmills are established in Bend.

Deschutes County is formed out of Crook County—the final county to be created in Oregon.

1920   National Prohibition goes into effect.

1926   Attempted bombing of state prohibition officers A.F. "Buck" Mariott and C.C. McBride takes place.

1933   Prohibition is repealed.

1946   Ochoco Hop ranch near Prineville is profiled by the *Bend Bulletin*—possibly the region's first commercial hop grower.

1950   Shevlin-Hixon sawmill is closed.

1958   Mount Bachelor ski resort is established.

1960   Olympia has 28.1 percent and Blitz-Weinhard 20.5 percent of Oregon beer sales.

1970   Blitz-Weinhard has 32.5 percent and Olympia 23.2 percent of Oregon beer sales, collectively leading the Oregon beer market.

1974   Larry Sidor joins Olympia Brewing.

1978   President Jimmy Carter signs into law legislation legalizing homebrewing.

1980   Bend population is 17,263.

1985   Don's Wines in downtown Bend offers homebrewing supplies for sale.

1986   John Harris is hired by McMenamins in 1986 to brew at the Hillsdale Pub.

1987   Gary Fish moves to Bend from Salt Lake City with plans to open a brewpub.

1988   Deschutes Brewery is opened to the public.

Deschutes Brewery introduces "Jubel-Ale" in 750ml bottles for winter seasonal. (In later years, the beer would be named "Jubelale.")

Deschutes' "Dark Winter" of infections leads to reworking of the brewhouse configuration.

1990   Bend population is 20,469.

Deschutes begins bottling Jubelale in twenty-two-ounce bottles.

1992   John Harris leaves Deschutes Brewery and begins brewing for Full Sail Brewing.

Scott Woehle establishes the Home Brewer homebrew supply shop.

Deschutes Brewery breaks ground on its planned production brewery expansion.

1993   Dr. Bill Pengelly is hired at Deschutes Brewery.

Deschutes Brewery production plant is opened; the first bottled beer off the bottling line is this year's Jubelale.

1994   Cascade Lakes Brewing is established as a production brewery in Redmond by David and Steven Gazeley.

Brooks-Scanlon sawmill is closed.

1995   Bend Brewing Company is established by Jerry Fox and Dave Hill; they are joined by Wendi Day as assistant manager. The brewer is Scott Saulsbury.

1996   Cascade Lakes Brewing opens the Seventh Street Brew House in Redmond; Jack Harris takes over brewing duties.

Tim Gossack departs Deschutes Brewery; Dr. Bill Pengelly is promoted to director of brewing.

Dan Pedersen takes over brewing duties at Bend Brewing.

Paul Arney is hired on at Deschutes Brewery.

1997   Larry Johnson buys the Home Brewer.

Larry Sidor departs Olympia Brewing and starts with S.S. Steiner in Yakima, Washington.

1998   Christian Skovborg takes over brewing duties from Dan Pedersen.

1999   Deschutes Brewery completes additional expansion at the production facility.

Mark Vickery departs Deschutes Brewery.

Tyler Reichert buys the Home Brewer.

2000   Bend population is 52,029.

Wendi Day purchases Bend Brewing Company from Jerry Fox and Dave Hill with partner Terry Standly.

Tyler Reichert moves the Home Brewer to its Division Street location.

McMenamins takes out a two-year option to purchase St. Francis School and announces plans to renovate the property.

Tyler Reichert receives the brewery license for Silver Moon Brewing.

2001   Cascade Lakes is purchased by Doug Kutella and Ray Orazetti.

Tyler Reichert launches Silver Moon Brewing.

Tony Lawrence departs Deschutes Brewery.

McMenamins meets with neighborhood representatives to discuss plans and set limits on traffic.

2002 McMenamins receives the go-ahead to move forward with its renovation plans of St. Francis School.

Chris Justema joins Kutella and Orazetti as partner in Cascade Lakes Brewing.

Tonya Cornett is hired as head brewer of Bend Brewing Company, replacing Christian Skovborg.

Paul Arney departs Deschutes Brewery.

2003 McMenamins closes the deal to buy St. Francis School property; it encounters delays later in the year.

Dr. Bill Pengelly departs from Deschutes Brewery.

Chris and Jeremy Cox purchase Lucy's Place, changing the name to JC's Bar and Grill.

2004 Larry Sidor starts as the new brewmaster at Deschutes Brewery.

Inaugural Bend Brew Fest takes place.

McMenamins Old St. Francis School is opened, with Dave Fleming as brewer.

Silver Moon Brewing and the Brew Shop move to Greenwood Avenue location; Tyler West is head brewer.

Paul Arney returns to Deschutes Brewery.

2005 Former Deschutes brewer Mark Henion joins Cascade Lakes Brewing.

Wanderlust Tours adds a beer tour to its lineup of guided outdoor tours.

First Bend Oktoberfest takes place.

2006 Mike White becomes the new brewer at McMenamins.

Bend Brewing wins its first GABF medal (gold), for HopHead Imperial IPA.

Wildfire Brewing is founded by the Cox brothers and former Deschutes brewer Paul Cook.

Deschutes Brewery introduces Hop Henge, The Abyss and Inversion IPA.

Tumalo Hops Company is established.

2007   Wildfire begins brewing.

Wade Underwood announces plans to build a brewpub in Sisters.

Tyler Reichert sells the Brew Shop to Tom Gilles.

Cascade Lakes removes the tasting room from the production brewery.

2008   Ground is broken on Three Creeks Brewing in Sisters.

Tonya Cornett wins Champion Brewmaster at World Beer Cup, becoming the first female brewer to do so.

Deschutes Brewery opens Portland Pub and celebrates its twentieth anniversary.

Three Creeks Brewing is opened, with Dave Fleming as head brewer.

Wildfire Brewing is required to change its name, revealed to be "10 Barrel Brewing."

Brewtal Brewing, later to become Boneyard, is announced by Tony Lawrence.

2009   Paul Cook leaves 10 Barrel for Ninkasi Brewing; Dan Olsen and Thom Tash join the brewing staff.

Tony Lawrence partners with Clay and Melodee Storey.

Mark Henion leaves Cascade Lakes for Ninkasi Brewing; John Van Duzer, formerly from Deschutes, takes over as head brewer.

10 Barrel announces plans to build a pub.

Inaugural Little Woody Barrel-Aged Brew Festival takes place.

Brett Thomas joins Silver Moon as assistant brewer.

The Abbey Pub is opened.

2010 First Silipint is created.

10 Barrel opens its west-side Bend Pub.

Bend Ale Trail is introduced.

Boneyard brews its first official beer.

Noble Brewing is announced, later to become GoodLife Brewing.

Old Mill Brew Wërks is announced.

Below Grade Brewing is announced.

Inaugural Sisters Fresh Hop Festival takes place.

Larry Johnson buys the original five-barrel brew system from Boneyard.

2011 Cascade Lakes remodels and expands its brewery.

Brewers Jimmy Seifrit and Paul Arney leave Deschutes Brewery.

10 Barrel hires Jimmy Seifert and Tonya Cornett.

Cycle Pub debuts at Bend WinterFest.

Deschutes Brewery begins expansion project on its Bend pub.

Solstice Brewing in Prineville is announced, opens a pub initially.

GoodLife Brewing opens for business.

Paul Arney announces departure from Deschutes to start his own brewery.

Larry Sidor announces plans to leave Deschutes in January 2012 to start his own brewery.

Below Grade Brewing debuts beers at NorthWest Crossing farmers' market.

Worthy Brewing is officially announced.

Groundbreaking begins on 10 Barrel's new fifty-barrel brewery.

Inaugural Whole Foods Brewfest takes place.

Phat Matt's Brewing in Redmond begins brewing.

Rat Hole Brewing is first announced.

The Brew Shop moves to Third Street, opens up Platypus Pub in the basement.

The Abbey Pub is closed and sold.

2012   Deschutes Brewery Bend Pub is closed for a month for remodeling and reopens in February.

10 Barrel Brewing hires Shawn Kelso and opens a new fifty-barrel production brewery.

Broken Top Bottle Shop opens in the former Abbey Pub location.

Old Mill Brew Wërks original owners sell the pub to focus on the brewery.

Tyler West announces departure from Silver Moon Brewing; Brett Thomas takes over as head brewer.

Paul Arney's the Ale Apothecary is officially in operation.

Boneyard Brewing signs a lease on a larger location to house a fifty-barrel brewery.

The Growler Guys open, becoming the first growler fill station in Oregon.

Inaugural Central Oregon Beer Week takes place.

Sunriver Brewing is announced and is open by the summer (beers are contract-brewed by Phat Matt's).

Worthy Brewing has its groundbreaking.

Smith Rock Brewing is announced in Redmond.

First mention of Larry Johnson's Shade Tree Brewing.

Inaugural Fermentation Celebration in the Old Mill District takes place.

The Crux Fermentation Project grand opening takes place.

Smith Rock Brewing officially opens in the late fall.

Solstice Brewing in Prineville brews its first batch of beer.

2013   Worthy Brewing has its official opening.

Debut of Rat Hole Brewing beers.

GoodLife begins canning its beer, becoming the first in Central Oregon to do so.

Brett Thomas departs Silver Moon Brewing for Sunriver Brewing.

Silver Moon ownership changes are announced; it is purchased by James Watts and Matt Barrett.

Rat Hole Brewpub officially opens, in the location vacated by the Old Mill Brew Wërks pub as it moves to a larger space.

First mention and details of Oblivion Brewing, North Rim Brewing, Bridge 99 Brewery, Juniper Brewing and RiverBend Brewing.

Beers from Bridge 99 debut at Wubba's BBQ Shack.

Debut of Platypus Pub beer, brewed by Bridge 99 Brewery.

Debut of beers from RiverBend Brewing.

2014   Brett Thomas at Sunriver Brewing brews first beers in-house.

Juniper Brewing is officially opened in Redmond.

Wild Ride Brewing is officially opened in Redmond.

North Rim Brewing in Bend officially begins selling beer.

Phat Matt's is no longer in operation.

Smith Rock Hop Farm is established.

BIBLIOGRAPHY

Books

Acitelli, Tom. *The Audacity of Hops: The History of America's Craft Beer Revolution*. Chicago: Chicago Review Press, 2013.

Braly, David. *Crooked River Country: Wranglers, Rogues, and Barons*. Pullman: Washington State University Press, 2007.

Brogan, Phil F. *East of the Cascades*. Portland, OR: Binford & Mort, 1964.

Coe, Urling C. *Frontier Doctor: Observations on Central Oregon and the Changing West*. Corvallis: Oregon State University Press, 1996. Originally published in 1940.

Cottone, Vince. *Good Beer Guide: Breweries and Pubs of the Pacific Northwest*. Seattle, WA: Homestead Book Company, 1986.

Crook County Historical Society and A.R. Bowman Memorial Museum. *Echoes from Old Crook County*. Prineville, OR: Crook County Historical Society, 1991.

Crowell, James L. *Frontier Publisher: A Romantic Review of George Palmer Putnam's Career at* The Bend Bulletin, *1910–1914, with an Extended Epilogue*. Bend, OR: Maverick Publications, 2008.

Deschutes County Historical Society. *Bend: 100 Years of History*. Battle Ground, WA: Pediment Publishing, 2004.

————. *A History of the Deschutes Country in Oregon*. Redmond, OR: Midstate Printing, 1985.

Dodd, Hudson, Matthew Latterell, Lani MacCormack and Ina Zucker. *The Brewpub Explorer of the Pacific Northwest*. Medina, WA: Johnston Associates International, 1996.

Dunlop, Pete. *Portland Beer: Crafting the Road to Beervana*. Charleston, SC: The History Press, 2013.

Fountain, Sue A. *Too Cold to Snow: A Memoir*. Bend, OR: self-published, printed by CreateSpace, 2013.

Gray, Edward. *Roughing It on the Little Deschutes River, 1934–1944: A History of a Sawmill Camp and Its People*. Eugene, OR: K&M Printing and Lithographing, 1986.

Gribskov, Joyce. *Pioneer Spirits of Bend*. Bend, OR: Maverick Publications, 1980.

Hatton, Raymond R. *Bend in Central Oregon*. Portland, OR: Binford & Mort, 1978.

————. *High Desert of Central Oregon*. Portland, OR: Binford & Mort, 1977.

Jefferson County Historical Society. *The History of Jefferson County, Oregon*. Dallas, TX: Taylor Publishing Company, 1984.

Meier, Gary, and Gloria Meier. *Brewed in the Pacific Northwest: A History of Beer Making in Oregon and Washington*. Seattle, WA: Fjord Press, 1991.

Morrison, Lisa. *Craft Beers of the Pacific Northwest: A Beer Lover's Guide to Oregon, Washington, and British Columbia*. Portland, OR: Timber Press, 2011.

Ogle, Maureen. *Ambitious Brew: The Story of American Beer*. Orlando, FL: Harcourt, 2006.

Okrent, Daniel. *Last Call: The Rise and Fall of Prohibition*. New York: Scribner, 2010.

Osgood, Judy, ed. *Desert Sage Memories*. Bend, OR: Retired and Senior Volunteer Program (RSVP), 2002.

————. *The River Flows as the Mountains Watch*. Bend, OR: Retired and Senior Volunteer Program (RSVP), 2000.

Snyder, Keith. *Prineville Business History: 1868–1922*. Bend, OR: Maverick Publications, 2004.

Williams, Elsie Horn. *The Bend Country: Past to Present*. Virginia Beach, VA: Donning Company/Publishers, 1983, 1998.

ARTICLES

A special note regarding the Bulletin, *Central Oregon's longest-running newspaper: Google has an extensive online archive of scanned issues from 1903 to 1994, and this greatly facilitated my research. The* Bulletin's *own website has more recent archives available. For reasons of space, the specific articles used are not cited or listed here. Electronic versions of all articles are in my possession.*

Bernstein, Joshua M. "Around the Bend." *Imbibe Magazine.* http://www. imbibemagazine.com/Bend-Oregon-Beer.

Borchelt, Nathan. "Bend, Ore., the City You'll Love to Hate." *Washington Post*, October 5, 2012. http://www.washingtonpost.com/lifestyle/travel/bend-ore-the-city-youll-love-to-hate/2012/10/04/9a7e2f10-042e-11e2-91e7-2962c74e7738_story.html.

Burningham, Lucy. "Bend, Ore., a Brewer's Town." *New York Times*, April 20, 2012. http://www.nytimes.com/2012/04/22/travel/in-bend-ore-craft-brewing-is-booming.html.

Cantwell, Brian J. "Thanks to Thirsty Outdoors Lovers, Bustling Bend Is Awash in Beer." *Seattle Times*, March 24, 2012. http://seattletimes.com/html/travel/2017809710_trbend25.html.

Gregory, Ronald L. "Life in Railroad Logging Camps of the Shevlin-Hixon Company, 1916–1950." Paper published by the Oregon State University Department of Anthropology, Corvallis, Oregon, 2001.

Jacklet, Ben. "Bend's Economy Is Coming Back to Life." *Oregon Business*, June 22, 2011. http://www.oregonbusiness.com/articles/101-july-2011/5460-bends-economy-is-coming-back-to-life.

———. "Q&A: Gary Fish, Founder and CEO, Deschutes Brewery." *Oregon Business*, October 1, 2008. http://www.oregonbusiness.com/articles/20/253.

Keates, Nancy. "Secrets of a Blue-Ribbon Brewmaster." *Wall Street Journal*, September 3, 2011. http://online.wsj.com/news/articles/SB100014240 53111904199404576538340458467326.

Schuhmacher, Harry. "The Second Craft Beer Revolution: Will It Stick This Time?" *All About Beer* (January 23, 2013). http://allaboutbeer.com/article/the-second-craft-beer-revolution-will-it-stick-this-time.

Spiro, Josh. "Is the Beer Business Recession-Proof?" *Inc. Magazine* (September 4, 2009). http://www.inc.com/news/articles/2009/09/beer.html.

Yardley, William. "An Economic Lifeline of Barley and Hops." *New York Times*, May 5, 2012. http://www.nytimes.com/2012/05/06/us/an-economic-lifeline-of-barley-and-hops.html.

WEBSITES AND ONLINE RESOURCES

A special note regarding my own blogs, "The Brew Site" (http://www.thebrewsite.com) and "Hack Bend" (http://www.hackbend.com): I have been writing them since 2004 and 2006, respectively, and much of the contemporary history that appears in this book was documented on them over the past decade. Specific blog posts are not listed or cited here but are available in the archives online at each respective blog.

Blunt, Will. "Dr. Bill Pengelly, Deschutes Brewery Brewmaster." StarChefs. http://www.starchefs.com/features/star_brewers/html/deschute.shtml.

Brewing Rabble of Eastern Washington. "Portland Brewpubs." http://www.brewingrabble.com/portland/portland_brewpubs.txt.

Burchette, Jordan, and Lauren Passell. "8 Best Beer Towns in the USA." CNN. http://www.cnn.com/2013/05/06/travel/usa-beer-towns.

City of Bend. "Bend Area General Plan: Chapter 4: Population and Demographics (PDF)." http://www.bend.or.us/modules/showdocument.aspx?documentid=4076.

Engdahl, Emily. "Interview Series: In Depth with Jack Harris of Fort George." #pdxbeergeeks. http://www.pdxbeergeeks.com/2012/02/interview-series-in-depth-with-jack.html.

Indie Hops. "Profile of Tonya Cornett." http://www.indiehops.com/tonya_cornett.asp.

John, Finn J.D. "Bootlegger's Paradise: Oregon's Prohibition Adventures." Offbeat Oregon. http://offbeatoregon.com/1308a-rumrunners-moonshiners-and-speakeasies.html.

———. "'Oregon's Outback' Was a Real Moonshiner's Paradise in '20s." Offbeat Oregon. http://www.offbeatoregon.com/1203c-moonshiners-of-oregon-outback.html.

Johnson-Greenough, Ezra. "Larry Sidor Interview Part 2, with Deschutes' New Brewmaster Cam O' Connor." The New School. http://www.newschoolbeer.com/2012/03/larry-sidor-interview-part-2-with.html.

———. "Larry Sidor's Crux Fermentation Project—Exclusive Interview, Part 1." The New School. http://www.newschoolbeer.com/2012/03/larry-sidors-crux-fermentation-project.html.

LaMar, Ryan. "Prohibition in Portland and Oregon." The Beer Traveler. http://beer.ryasrealm.com/Prohibition.htm.

LaRowe, Alethea Smartt. "Barn to Brewpub: Rat Hole Sets Up Near Old Mill." Oregon Beer Growler. http://www.oregonbeergrowler.com/blog/-barn-to-brewpub-rat-hole-sets-up-near-old-mill.

Library of Congress. "An Illustrated History of Central Oregon (1905)." Archive.org. https://archive.org/details/illustratedhist00shav.

Lies, Mitch. "Hops Spread to Central Oregon." Capital Press. http://www.capitalpress.com/content/ml-tumalo-hops-100810-art.

Lut, Margaret. "Interview with Larry Sidor, Deschutes Brewmaster, Part 1." Brewpublic. http://brewpublic.com/beer-personalities/larrysidor.

———. "Interview with Larry Sidor, Deschutes Brewmaster, Part 2." Brewpublic. http://brewpublic.com/beer-personalities/larrysidorpart2.

Oberst, Gail. "Pioneering Woman: Wendi Day." Oregon Beer Growler. http://www.oregonbeergrowler.com/blog/pioneering-woman-wendi-day.

Oregon State Archives. "Prohibition in Oregon: The Vision and the Reality." Oregon State Archives 50th Anniversary Exhibit. http://arcweb.sos.state.or.us/pages/exhibits/50th/prohibition1/prohibintro.html.

Paul, D.J. "Golden Valley Restaurant & Brewery—Beaverton, Oregon." Brewpublic. http://brewpublic.com/brewpubs/21649.

United States Census. "10th Population Census of the United States—1880." Archive.org. https://archive.org/details/10thcensus1084unit.

———. "12th Population Census of the United States—1900." Archive.org. https://archive.org/details/12thcensusofpopu1346unit.

Visit Bend. "Bend Area Visitor Survey Summer 2013 Final Results." http://www.visitbend.com/Bend-Summer-2013-Report-FINAL-11-18-13.pdf.

INTERVIEWS

Most of these interviews were conducted in person and recorded. The recordings and transcripts of these interviews are in the possession of the author.

Barnett, Ty. Personal interview, March 20, 2014.

Cornett, Tonya. Personal interview, January 17, 2014.

Cox, Chris. Personal interview, January 17, 2014.

Fish, Gary. Personal interview, February 10, 2014.

Harris, John. Personal interview, March 10, 2014.

Justema, Chris. Personal interview, January 14, 2014.

Lawrence, Tony. Personal interview, April 5, 2014.

McMenamin, Brian. Personal interview, March 10, 2014.

Reichert, Tyler. Personal interview, January 7, 2014.

Seifrit, Jimmy. Personal interview, January 17, 2014.

Storey, Clay, and Melodee Storey. Personal interview, February 26, 2014.

Thomas, Brett. Personal interview, January 28, 2014.

Underwood, Wade. Personal interview, January 21, 2014.

Wales, Garrett. Personal interview, January 17, 2014.

Watts, James. Personal interview, May 8, 2014.

White, Mike. Personal interview, March 13, 2014.

INDEX

A

A1 Beer 25
Abbey Pub 141
Ale Apothecary 126
Anti-Saloon League 37, 39, 42
Appleton, Frank
  helped design Deschutes Brewery 77
  helped design Deschutes Brewery
    production brewhouse 81
Arney, Paul 89, 95, 97
  departs Deschutes Brewery to start
    the Ale Apothecary 118
  launches the Ale Apothecary 126

B

Barker, Joe. *See also* Solstice Brewing
    Company
Barnett, Ty 115, 116. *See* GoodLife
    Brewing Company
  manages restaurant in Cannon Beach 115
Barrett, Matt 134, 138. *See* Silver
    Moon Brewing
Bateman, Duane 76
  proposed brewery in old Skyliners
    Lodge 74

Below Grade Brewing 116
  debut at NorthWest Crossing farmers'
    market 120
Bend
  Bond Street 29, 38, 39, 41, 54
  Drake, Alexander 27, 30
  Farewell Bend Ranch 26
  Hedges, Henry 30, 145
  Sisemore, John 26
  Todd, John Y. 26
Bend Ale Trail 125, 131, 133, 137,
    140, 145
Bend Brew Fest 131, 142, 143
Bend Brewing Company 83, 89, 93,
    103, 117
  opens 86
Bergeman, Paul. *See* Wild Ride
    Brewing
BierBike (inspired the Cycle Pub) 138
Black Butte Porter. *See* Deschutes
    Brewery
Blitz-Weinhard Company
  advertising 63
  share of beer sales 65
Boller, Don. *See* Don's Wines
Boneyard Brewing 21, 95, 146

explosive growth 130
opens 112
RPM IPA, flagship beer 130
sells five-barrel system to Larry
    Johnson 122
Brewpub Bill 69, 70, 71
Brew Shop 67, 99, 103, 142
    relocates to larger space 123
    sold to Tom Gilles 106
Brewtal Brewing Company. *See*
    Boneyard Brewing
Brewtal Industries. *See* Lawrence, Tony
Bridge 99 Brewery 135
Broken Top Bottle Shop 142
Brooks-Scanlon sawmill 26, 51, 52, 67
Butschy, Darin. *See* Oblivion Brewing
    Company

C

Cameron, Brian. *See* Sunriver Brewing
    Company
Cascade Lakes Brewing Company 83,
    87, 89, 92, 102, 106, 112
    Cascade Lakes Lodge 93
    Seventh Street Brewhouse 88, 93
Central Oregon Beer Week 143
Central Oregon Homebrewers
    Organization 114, 141
Cook, Paul 96
    departs 10 Barrel Brewing 112
    departs Deschutes Brewery for
        Wildfire Brewing 105
Coors 70, 71
Cornett, Tonya 93, 130, 140, 146
    departs Bend Brewing for 10 Barrel
        Brewing 117
    GABF and World Beer Cup awards
        103
    sour and experimental beers 117
Cox, Chris and Jeremy 101. *See* 10
    Barrel Brewing Company
    establish Wildfire Brewing 105
craft beer industry growth 84
Crook County

Deschutes County formed from 51
first settlers 22
formed 22
goes dry under local option 40
Crux Fermentation Project 126
opens 130
temporarily named 856 Brewing 120
Cycle Pub 134, 138, 140

D

D and D Club 56
Dark Winter of 1988. *See* Deschutes
    Brewery
Day, Wendi
    hires Tonya Cornett 93
    manager of Bend Brewing Company
        86
    purchases Bend Brewing Company
        from her father 89
Deschutes Brewery 21, 69, 86, 102,
    109, 117, 146, 147
    Black Butte Porter recipe
        development 78, 84
    early expansion 80
    first-year infection ("Dark Winter")
        78
    Jubelale, winter warmer 79
    new production brewery online 84
    popularity of Black Butte Porter in
        Portland 80
    signs with Haines Distributing 80
Don's Wines (early homebrew supply)
    66, 83

E

856 Brewing. *See* Crux Fermentation
    Project
Endicott, Curtis. *See* Juniper Brewing
    Company
Evans, Ed (co-owner of Ochoco
    Brewery) 24
Evers, Paul 120. *See* Crux
    Fermentation Project

F

Fermentation Celebration 130, 144
Fischetti, Diana. *See* Broken Top Bottle
    Shop
Fish, Gary 69, 72, 73, 77, 78, 79, 80,
    81, 84, 147
  early struggles with brewpub 78
  helps launch Rubicon Brewing 72
  moves to Bend from Salt Lake City
    73
  troubles staffing brewpub 77
Fleming, Dave
  brewer at McMenamins Old St.
    Francis School 99
  brewer at Three Creeks Brewing
    108
Fox, Jerry (founder of Bend Brewing
    Company) 83, 86, 89. *See also*
    Bend Brewing Company
  hires daughter Wendi Day to manage
    Bend Brewing 86
frontier breweries 23

G

Gazeley, Steve and Dave 87
  launch Cascade Lakes Brewing
    Company 83
  sell Cascade Lakes Brewing 92
Geiger, John (brewer at Prineville
    Brewery) 25
Gilles, Tom, purchases the Brew Shop
    106
GoodLife Brewing Company 120, 126,
    130
  announced as Noble Brewing 115
  changes name from Noble Brewing
    120
  first brewery in Central Oregon to
    can its beers 132
Gossack, Tim 80, 82
  departs Deschutes for Rio Salado
    Brewing 89
  took over as head brewer of
    Deschutes 81

Growler Guys 139
growlers 79, 139, 140

H

Harris, Jack 88. *See also* Cascade Lakes
    Brewing Company
Harris, John 75, 77, 78, 80
  departs Deschutes Brewery for Full
    Sail Brewing 81
  enlisted by Duane Bateman for
    possible Bend brewery 75
  McMenamins recipe development 76
Hawman, Trever. *See* Bridge 99
    Brewery
Healy, Bill (founder of Mount Bachelor
    resort) 60
Healy, Cameron. *See* Healy, Bill
  helps start Kona Brewing 61
Henion, Mark 89
  departs Cascade Lakes Brewing 112
  departs Deschutes Brewery for
    Cascade Lakes Brewing 102
  takes over as head brewer at
    Deschutes Brewery 96
Hill, Dave 83, 86
  founder of Bend Brewing Company.
    See Bend Brewing Company
Home Brewer
  homebrew supply shop 67, 83, 90,
    122
  purchased by Tyler Reichert 90
homebrewing 46, 66, 89, 90
hops 23, 66, 128, 143, 145
  early regional cultivation 30, 145

J

JC's Bar and Grill 101, 105
Johnson, Larry 90, 122, 136
  launches Shade Tree Brewing 130
  purchases the Home Brewer 90
  Shade Tree Brewing. *See* Shade Tree
    Brewing
Jubelale. *See* Deschutes Brewery
Juniper Brewing Company 135

Justema, Chris 89, 102
  joins as partner at Cascade Lakes
    Brewing 92
JV Northwest
  builds Deschutes Brewery's fifty-barrel
    brewhouse 81
  builds twenty-five-barrel system for
    Cascade Lakes Brewing 113

K

Kelso, Shawn. *See* 10 Barrel Brewing
    Company
Kemph, Tom 89. *See also* Cascade
    Lakes Brewing Company
Kennedy, Chad 122, 128, 130
  Worthy Brewing. *See* Worthy Brewing
    Company
Kennedy, Jim, helped launch Deschutes
    Brewery beers in Portland 80
Kutella, Doug 92, 93
  Cascade Lakes Brewing. *See* Cascade
    Lakes Brewing Company

L

Lancaster, Lorren
  brewer at Silver Moon Brewing 113
  co-founds Old Mill Brew Werks with
    David Love 116
  departs Old Mill Brew Werks 116
La Pine 32
Larkin, Ian 118. *See also* Bend Brewing
    Company
Lawrence, Tony 80, 82, 109, 113
  Brewtal Industries consulting
    company 110
  departs Deschutes Brewery 95
  partners with Clay and Melodee
    Storey 111
Lesmeister, Scott. *See* Juniper Brewing
    Company
Little Woody Barrel-Aged Brew Fest
    132, 143
Loacker, Frank (first owner of Ochoco
    Brewery) 24

local option 29, 40, 41. *See also*
    Prohibition
  bill passed in Oregon 40
  Crook County goes dry 40
  Crook County goes wet again 40
Log Cabin Saloon 29
Logsdon, Dave, helps troubleshoot
    Deschutes infection issues 78
Love, David 116. *See also* Old Mill
    Brew Werks
Lucy's Place (bar purchased by Chris
    and Jeremy Cox) 101

M

Madras 30, 32, 39
Marlowe, Geoff. *See* Abbey Pub
McMahon, Michael 121. *See also* Old
    Mill Brew Werks
McMenamin, Brian 70, 76, 114
McMenamins 70, 88, 91, 131
  Hillsdale Pub, first post-Prohibition
    brewpub in Oregon 71
  hired John Harris as third brewer 75
  influence on Chris and Jeremy Cox 102
  influence on Wade Underwood 107
  Old St. Francis School 104, 114
  renovating St. Francis School 97
Miles, Asa (co-owner of Ochoco
    Brewery) 24
Mitchell, Brian. *See* Wild Ride Brewing
moonshine 35, 42
Mount Bachelor 60, 73, 80
Mulder, Matt. *See* Phat Matt's Brewing
    Company

N

Neel Distributing 65
Neilsen, Shane. *See* North Rim
    Brewing Company
Noble Brewing Company. *See*
    GoodLife Brewing Company
North Rim Brewing Company 136

O

Oblivion Brewing Company 134
Ochoco Brewery 24, 26
O'Kane, Hugh 29, 97
Old Mill Brew Wërks 116, 120, 126
  relocates brewpub to larger space
    133
Old Mill District 26
Old St. Francis School 102, 104, 108,
    114, 131
  opened in 1936 99
  purchased by McMenamins 92
  undergoing renovations by
    McMenamins 97
Olsen, Dan
  brewer at 10 Barrel Brewing 112
  departs 10 Barrel to brew at
    RiverBend Brewing 135
Olympia Brewing
  advertising 63
  beer popular on the frontier 29
  Larry Sidor joins 96
O'Neil, George (owner of Prineville
    Brewery) 24
O'Neil Saloon (owned by George
    O'Neil) 24
Orazetti, Rick 92, 93
  Cascade Lakes Brewing. See Cascade
    Lakes Brewing Company
Oregon Liquor Control Commission
    117, 122, 131, 139

P

Palace 54, 62
Pedersen, Dan 87. See also Bend
    Brewing Company
  leaves Bend Brewing Company 89
Pengelly, Dr. Bill 82
  leaves Deschutes Brewery 96
  takes over as director of brewing at
    Deschutes 89
Phat Matt's Brewing Company 122,
    126, 130
  out of business 136

Plants, Curt 115, 116. See also
    GoodLife Brewing Company
  works with John Maier at Rogue 115
Platypus Pub 123, 135, 142
Polanchek, Andy. See Broken Top
    Bottle Shop
Powell, Jason and Jennifer. See Broken
    Top Bottle Shop
Prineville 21, 22, 24, 31, 32, 121
  Ochoco Hop Ranch 145
  Prine, Barney 22
Prineville Brewery 24, 25, 29
Prohibition 29, 32
  ardent spirits law 37
  death of Vayle Taylor 45
  dynamiting of Congress apartments
    35
  local option 29, 40, 41
  measure of 1914 41
  officers A.F. "Buck" Mariott and C.C.
    McBride 35, 45
  repealed 49

R

Rather, Pratt. See GoodLife Brewing
    Company
Rat Hole Brewing 122, 126, 132
  announced 132
  opened brewpub 134
Redmond 30, 32, 38, 66, 83, 122
Reichert, Tyler 90, 99, 103, 113, 114,
    117
  acquires brewing equipment from
    Bandon 91
  purchases the Home Brewer 90
Riggs, Josh. See Phat Matt's Brewing
    Company
RiverBend Brewing Company 135
RPM IPA. See Boneyard Brewing

S

Saulsbury, Scott 86. See also Bend
    Brewing Company
  departs Bend Brewing Company 87

Seifrit, Jimmy 89, 118, 130
  departs Deschutes Brewery for 10
    Barrel Brewing 117
Shade Tree Brewing 122, 130, 136
Sheehan, Father Luke, established St.
    Francis Catholic school 97
Sidor, Larry 96, 102, 117, 118, 130
  departs Deschutes Brewery 118
  launches Crux Fermentation Project
    126
Silipint (collapsible silicone pint glass) 140
Silver Moon Brewing 103, 106, 112,
    113, 116, 117, 134
  contract-brewing for Old Mill Brew
    Wërks 120
  how it was named 91
  moves downtown 99
  sold 134
Sisters 21, 33, 106
Sisters Brewing Company (possible
    early brewery in Sisters) 107
Sisters Fresh Hop Festival 132, 143
Skovborg, Christian 89. See also Bend
    Brewing Company
  departs Bend Brewing Company 94
Skyliners Lodge 60, 74
Smith Rock Brewing 130
Solstice Brewing Company 122, 126
  first Prineville brewery since the
    frontier days 121
  installs in-house brewing equipment
    130
Storey, Clay and Melodee 110. See also
    Boneyard Brewing
Sunriver Brewing Company 126, 134,
    135
  opens 130

T

Tash, Thom 112. See also 10 Barrel
    Brewing Company
Taylor, Evan 103. See also Silver Moon
    Brewing
  departs Silver Moon Brewing 113

10 Barrel Brewing Company 21, 71,
    112, 117, 128, 135, 138, 146
  breaks ground on new production
    brewery 118
  changed name from Wildfire Brewing
    109
Thomas, Brett
  brewer with Silver Moon Brewing
    114
  brews first beers in-house at Sunriver
    Brewing 135
  departs Silver Moon Brewing for
    Sunriver Brewing 134
  takes over head brewer position at
    Silver Moon Brewing 128
Three Creeks Brewing Company 108,
    109, 125, 143
Toepfer, Al 122, 126, 132. See also Rat
    Hole Brewing
Tumalo Hops Company 145
Tumalo Tavern 92

U

Underwood, Wade 106, 143. See
    also Three Creeks Brewing
    Company

V

Van Duzer, John 89, 103
  takes over as head brewer at Cascade
    Lakes Brewing 113
Vickery, Mark 80, 82
  departs Deschutes for Golden Valley
    Brewery 89
Visit Bend 125, 131, 137

W

Wales, Brad
  owner of Bachelor Beverage
    Company 71
  partner in 10 Barrel Brewing 109
Wales, Garrett (partner in 10 Barrel
    Brewing) 109

Wanderlust Tours 131, 137
Watts, James (founder of Cycle Pub)
        134, 138
West, Tyler 91, 114. *See* Silver Moon
        Brewing
  becomes head brewer at Silver Moon
        Brewing 99
  departs Silver Moon Brewing 128
White, Mike 114
  brewer at McMenamins Old St.
        Francis School 104
Wildfire Brewing Company 105, 106,
        109
  changes name to 10 Barrel Brewing
        109
  contract-brewed first Three Creeks
        beers 108
Wild Ride Brewing 135
Wilson, Dave 120. *See* Crux
        Fermentation Project
Wise, Dean 117, 120. *See* Below Grade
        Brewing
Woehle, Scott (opens the Home
        Brewer) 83, 90
Woman's Christian Temperance Union
        37, 39
  Rachel Ellis 39
Worthington, Roger (owner of Worthy
        Brewing) 122, 128
Worthy Brewing Company 128, 130
  groundbreaking ceremony 128
  official opening 132
  planned for Bend's east side 122

ABOUT THE AUTHOR

Jon Abernathy has been blogging about craft beer for more than a decade and drinking and homebrewing it for far longer. Having grown up in Central Oregon, Jon went to school in Spokane, Washington, graduating from Eastern Washington University with a bachelor's degree in French and ultimately began working in the computer industry as a web developer after returning to Bend. Blogging was a natural outlet for a web developer with a love of writing (and beer), and in 2004, Jon launched "The Brew Site," a blog dedicated to all things beer and brewing. The blog has gone on to become the longest-running American beer blog and has documented the change and rapid growth that has characterized the Bend and Central Oregon brewing scene. You can visit "The Brew Site" at www.thebrewsite.com, as well as the companion website to this book at www.bendbeerhistory.com.